Monographs of the
Hebrew Union College,
Number 7

Secular Education in
Philo of Alexandria

An I. Edward Kiev
Library Foundation Book

Alan Mendelson

Secular Education
in Philo of Alexandria

Hebrew Union College Press
Cincinnati 1982

© Copyright 1982 by the Hebrew Union College Press
Hebrew Union College-Jewish Institute of Religion

Library of Congress Cataloging in Publication Data

Mendelson, Alan.
  Secular education in Philo of Alexandria.

  (Monographs of the Hebrew Union College, ISSN 0190-
5627 ; no. 7)
  Bibliography: p.
  Includes index.
  1. Philo, of Alexandria—Education. 2. Education,
Ancient—Philosophy. 3. Jews—Education—Philosophy.
4. Hellenism. I. Title. II. Series.
LB85.P452M46   370'.1   82-886
ISBN 0-87820-406-7   AACR2

Designed by Noel Martin
Manufactured in the United States of America
Distributed by KTAV Publishing House, Inc.
New York, New York 10013

To the memory of
Lex Aronson
born 20 December 1934
שהלך לעולמו עקה"ש

I. Edward Kiev Library Foundation

In memory of Dr. I. Edward Kiev, alike distinguished as Rabbi, Chaplain and Librarian of the Hebrew Union College-Jewish Institute of Religion in New York, his family and friends have established in September 1976 a Library Foundation bearing his name, to support and encourage the knowledge, understanding and appreciation of books, manuscripts and other efforts of scholars in Judaica and Hebraica. In cooperation with the Faculty Publications Committee of the Hebrew Union College-Jewish Institute of Religion the Foundation offers the present volume as the second I. Edward Kiev Library Foundation Volume.

Contents

Preface

More than a decade ago, Professor Louis H. Feldman of Yeshiva University remarked to me that the subject of education in Philo was yet unexplored. Proceeding on this hint, I wrote a dissertation on the subject in the Committee on the History of Culture at the University of Chicago. The chairman of that Committee, Professor Karl J. Weintraub, suspended his disbelief while the idea took hold. I shall always be grateful to him for his indulgence and his academic concern. The dissertation, written under the guidance of Professors R. M. Grant and J. Z. Smith, was finished in 1971 ("Encyclical Education in Philo of Alexandria").

A period of *Wanderjahre* ensued. From 1971–73 I taught at Hebrew University of Jerusalem. During that time, I received many helpful suggestions from Professor S. Daniel and again from Professor Feldman. I then moved to Oxford, England, where Mr. Gregory desJardins was kind enough to comment thoroughly on the manuscript. But it was not until I came to Canada in 1976 that I was able to pull the threads together. The resulting monograph has evolved considerably from the original, and I am indebted to all the people mentioned here for prodding me to explore new avenues which the rich material of Philo continues to provide.

While at McMaster University, I have been working with a team of scholars who are studying the process whereby Jews and Christians in the ancient world moved towards explicit definitions of what it meant to hold their respective faiths. This study is supported by the Social Sciences and Humanities Research Council of Canada, and I have a major debt of gratitude to that institution for providing a stimulating atmosphere in which to work. I am particularly grateful to the coordinator of the program, Professor E. P. Sanders, for encouraging this study and for many acts of kindness. I should like to thank Dr. A. I. Baumgarten, Dr. Tamar Frank, Dr. William Gerber, Professor David Winston, and especially the late Professor Samuel Sandmel. The role of Hebrew Union College in the publication of this monograph is a tale in itself. Let me only record here my deepest appreciation to and respect for Professor Michael A. Meyer, Chairman of the Publications Committee, and three perceptive readers: Professors Carl R. Holladay and Ben Zion Wacholder and Mr. William A. Hartfelder, Jr. I should also express my thanks to Harvard University Press for permission to use their translations of Philo in the Loeb Classical Library.

Over the course of the years, I received invaluable bibliographical aid from Professor Earle Hilgert of the Philo Institute. On several occasions, Professor Peder Borgen and Roald Skarsten of the University of Trondheim, Norway, provided me with print-out from their key-word-in-context Concordance to Philo. I would also like to thank Mrs. Grace Gordon and Ms. Phyllis DeRosa Koetting for typing the manuscript with such good cheer.

Finally, there are the members of my family without whose encouragement this monograph literally would not have seen the light of day. I dedicated the dissertation to my wife Sara in gratitude for the substantive contributions she made. In the intervening years, she has continued, with deepening insight, to make such contributions. In other times, I would have dedicated this work to her as a token of my appreciation which cannot be expressed in other words. But in 1975, while we were living in the quiet of Oxford, a friend of many years went to Kurdistan to render humanitarian aid to the victims of war. He was imprisoned by the Iraqi authorities on false charges and was executed. It is to him that the dedication belongs.

Abbreviations of Philonic Works

Unless otherwise indicated, the text and translation of Philo used is from the Loeb Classical Library edition prepared by G. H. Whitaker, F. H. Colson, and R. Marcus (10 vols.; 2 supplementary vols.; London, 1929–53). Numbers in parentheses refer to the Loeb volume in which the particular work appears.

Abr.	*De Abrahamo.* (6)
Aet.	*De Aeternitate Mundi.* (9)
Agr.	*De Agricultura.* (3)
Cher.	*De Cherubim.* (2)
Conf.	*De Confusione Linguarum.* (4)
Cong.	*De Congressu quaerendae Eruditionis gratia.* (4)
Cont.	*De Vita Contemplativa.* (9)
Decal.	*De Decalogo.* (7)
Det.	*Quod Deterius Potiori insidiari solet.* (2)
Ebr.	*De Ebrietate.* (3)
Flac.	*In Flaccum.* (9)
Fug.	*De Fuga et Inventione.* (5)
Gig.	*De Gigantibus.* (2)
Heres	*Quis Rerum Divinarum Heres.* (4)
Hypoth.	*Hypothetica.* (9)
Immut.	*Quod Deus immutabilis sit.* (3)
Jos.	*De Iosepho.* (6)
LA i, ii, iii	*Legum Allegoriae* i, ii, iii. (1)
Legat.	*De Legatione ad Gaium.* (10)
Mig.	*De Migratione Abrahami.* (4)
*Mos.*i, ii	*De Vita Mosis* i, ii. (6)
Mut.	*De Mutatione Nominum.* (5)
Opif.	*De Opificio Mundi.* (1)
Plant.	*De Plantatione.* (3)
Post.	*De Posteritate Caini.* (2)
Praem.	*De Praemiis et Poenis.* (8)
Prob.	*Quod Omnis Probus Liber sit.* (9)
Provid.	*De Providentia.* (9)
QE i, ii	*Quaestiones et Solutiones in Exodum* i, ii. (Suppl. 2)
QG i, ii, iii, iv	*Quaestiones et Solutiones in Genesin* i, ii, iii, iv. (Suppl. 1)

Sac.   *De Sacrificiis Abelis et Caini.* (2)

Sob.   *De Sobrietate.* (3)

Som. i, ii   *De Somniis* i, ii. (5)

Spec. i, ii, iii, iv   *De Specialibus Legibus* i, ii, iii, iv. (7,8)

Virt.   *De Virtutibus.* (8)

Other Abbreviations

Journals and standard works in Philonic scholarship are abbreviated only when they are cited frequently.

CP   *Classical Philology*

CPJ   *Corpus papyrorum Judaicorum,* ed. Victor A. Tcherikover and Alexander Fuks. 3 vols. Cambridge, 1957–64.

HTR   *Harvard Theological Review*

HUCA   *Hebrew Union College Annual*

JBL   *Journal of Biblical Literature*

JQR   *Jewish Quarterly Review*

JTS   *Journal of Theological Studies*

LCL   *Loeb Classical Library*

PAL   *Philon d'Alexandrie, Lyon 11–16 Septembre 1966: Colloque,* ed. R. Arnaldez, C. Mondésert, and J. Pouilloux. Paris: Édition du Centre national de la recherche scientifique, 1967.

PLCL   *Philo Loeb Classical Library*

TDNT   *Theological Dictionary of the New Testament,* ed. G. Kittel, G. Friedrich. 9 vols. Grand Rapids, 1964–1974.

Introduction

The encounter of Judaism and Hellenism in the Fertile Crescent has long captured the imagination. The alleged meeting between Aristotle and a Jew, originally recorded by Clearchus of Soli (ca. 300 B.C.E.) and reiterated by Josephus, Clement of Alexandria, and Eusebius, epitomizes this confrontation.[1] Whatever the historical truth of that meeting, there is something compelling about the image; indeed the encounter seems to have an epic dimension. In Clearchus' reconstruction, Aristotle says:

> Now this man [a Jew of Coele-Syria], who was entertained by a large circle of friends and was on his way from the interior to the coast, not only spoke Greek, but had the soul of a Greek. During my stay in Asia, he visited the same places as I did, and came to converse with me and some other scholars, to test our learning. But as one who had been intimate with many cultivated persons, it was rather he who imparted to us something of his own (Josephus, *Contra Apionem*, I, 180–81).[2]

Several avenues of approach are open to those studying the extent to which Hellenism permeated Judaism. One can study Greek remains in the material culture of Palestine. As Tcherikover points out: "Excavations carried out during the last thirty years at various places in [Palestine] and in Transjordan have revealed that Greek influence began to penetrate as early as the seventh century B.C.E., while in the fifth and fourth centuries it reached very wide proportions."[3] Later literary and papyrological evidence indicates that Jews adopted Greek names—both in Palestine and the Diaspora.[4] Greek also appears prominently on Jewish funerary monuments in Palestine,[5] and Lieberman's classic works on the encounter of Judaism and Hellenism fill out the picture.[6] From the world of commerce to that of the Talmud, Greek appears not only in evidence, but in high relief.

But let us backtrack for a moment and ask how deep the penetration was. The presence of Attic artifacts in Palestine is significant; yet, as Tcherikover himself notes, in the period before Alexander's Conquest the brief encounters between Greeks and Jews "led to no cultural fusion."[7] The use of Greek on Jewish tombstones in Beth She'arim may indicate a general ignorance of Hebrew without proving any influence more profound.[8] In the same vein, we should recall that among the numerous Greek loan words in the Midrash, Mishnah, and Talmud,[9] Wolfson was not able to identify one technical term from Greek philosophy.[10] Yet, the passage from Clearchus of Soli intimates in a tantalizing manner that there were Jews who embraced the legacy of Greece more profoundly.

The fusion of Judaism and Hellenism actually reached its acme not in Palestine, but in Alexandria. The tradition linking the composition of the

Septuagint to the city of Alexandria bears witness to the extent to which Greek had taken hold there. Philo, who represents the culmination of such hellenizing currents upon Alexandrian Jewry, does not apologize when he uses the Greek translation of Scripture. On the contrary, he goes out of his way to give it authority equal to the Hebrew (*Mos.* ii.31–40), and his Biblical interpretations are based on the Greek text. We may suppose, then, that whether or not Philo knew Hebrew, his readers and co-religionists in the first century C.E. in Alexandria were most comfortable with the Septuagint and Philo's interpretations of that text.

One indication of Philo's Hellenism may be seen in his use of a language, once alien to his people, to elucidate Scripture. But Philo did not simply use Greek; he also borrowed substantive points from Greek philosophy to solve problems which the Torah presented. We may see an illustration of this in a question which arises early in the book of Genesis: why are there two accounts of the Creation? In *De Opificio Mundi* Philo answers in detail and without hesitation, giving the Platonic distinction that the first creation is the intelligible world of forms, whereas the second is the sensible world of material objects. In fact, Philo turns to Plato so often and on points of such importance that we may draw only one conclusion: Philo's dependence on Greek philosophy was not merely a matter of convenience; it was rather a question of conviction. Whether Philo's audience in Alexandria had actually *read* Plato is not the issue here. It is more important to observe that, for Philo and presumably for his readers, Greek philosophy filled Scripture with new meaning. This is one of the signs of profound fusion between Judaism and Hellenism.

Philo's appropriation of Greek culture was by no means uncritical. At some points Philo sounds as if he were an advocate of a specific philosophical school.[11] Then he will abruptly shift his ground, and the reader will find himself in an opposing philosophical camp. Philo's penchant for choosing among his philosophical predecessors may, at first, seem bewildering, but his allegiance to one Greek thinker or another is rarely arbitrary. Even though Philo does not always give explicit reasons for his appropriations or rejections of Greek philosophy, his commitment to Judaism certainly influenced his choices.

In analyzing the Jewish component of Philo's thought, it might be helpful to think in terms of a basic core of beliefs, a bare minimum without which Philo would not have recognized himself as a Jew. I do not intend to introduce here a "native Judaism" in Wolfson's sense of the term,[12] that is, a broad collection of beliefs both past and future, ideal and real. I allude, rather, to the narrowest possible set of beliefs without which Jewish life in Alexandria would have lost its meaning for Philo. From this core some traditional ("rabbinic") Jewish beliefs may have been pruned away because Philo, reflecting three centuries of Jewish life in the Diaspora, no longer sees them as central to his life as a Jew.[13] Other beliefs which come closer to Philo's definition of him-self as a Jew are held with great tenacity.[14] It is for the latter beliefs that Philo seeks and finds philosophical justifications, or at least rational explanations. Whenever an issue approaches the core of Philo's existence as a Jew, philo-sophy becomes a handmaiden to Scripture, and Scripture determines the course of Philo's thought.

Having set forth in a theoretical way some of the factors which influence appropriation or rejection of any given "alien" element, I should like to give an illustration of Philo's rejection of a Greek cultural ideal. Philo condemns homosexuality in *Abr.* 135–36 and *Spec.* iii.37–42. These passages are in har-mony with Biblical injunctions such as Lev. 18:22 and 20:13, and it is not dif-ficult to see Philo's rejection of homosexuality growing directly out of Scrip-ture. Now Philo might have cited the passages from Leviticus and stopped there. This he does not do because he is keenly involved in the process of appropriation and rejection of Hellenism. Since Philo is so concerned with any practice which has a Greek flavor, in *Cont.* 59–62 Philo takes his quarrel with homosexuality and lays it at Plato's door. The bone of contention becomes the *Symposium* itself. Philo reads that work—wrongly, I believe—as favoring homosexuality. Flying in the face of his philosophical mentor, Philo rejects the *Symposium* even though that dialogue, as it culminates in Diotima's speech, does not "endorse" the practice of homosexuality.[15]

Whenever Philo appropriates with modifications or rejects part of the legacy of Greece he is drawing a line. Beyond this point, we can imagine him saying, I will not go. The process of line-drawing is implicit throughout the present work; occasionally it is made explicit. This monograph deals with one instance of cautious appropriation—Philo's appropriation of secular or encyclical education (from the Greek *enkyklios paideia*). Put in more modern terms, I shall be investigating how the liberal arts and sciences fared in Philo's thought. At the outset it should be clear that, by limiting myself to one Greek concept which Philo chose to make his own, I shall explore in depth only one aspect of Philo's complex response to Hellenism. It should be borne in mind, though, that appropriation and rejection are two sides of the same coin. Viewed from either perspective, what is at stake is a man's creative adaptation to his environment.

As I have indicated, Philo weighed every alien concept, accepting some, modifying others, and rejecting still others. This course of action lies between two extreme positions. One extreme is to reject everything which bears the taint of Hellenism. During the Hellenistic period, especially in Palestine, there were Jews who adopted this position. Philo indicates that even in Alexandria some Jews tried to do likewise. The other extreme is to adopt an alien culture uncritically and without reservation. This path was particularly attractive to well-educated Jews with cosmopolitan aspirations. Since by all accounts Alexandria had a vibrant pagan culture, this option was a temptation to Jews in Philo's circle. Indeed Philo's nephew, Tiberius Julius Alexander, actually took the path into apostasy.[16] The difference between Philo and his nephew is the difference between accommodation with another culture and assimilation in that culture. Philo weighed concepts and drew lines in relation to the core of his Jewish beliefs. Philo's ruling passion was to make a grand synthesis of the two traditions he knew.

Assimilation has been a live option to Jews in many times and in many lands. Philo's choice not to exercise this option is a poignant moment in the cultural survival of Judaism.

I have spoken mainly in the abstract about the appropriation and rejection of certain cultural phenomena. In practical terms, a very basic problem arises. Scholars might agree that appropriation has taken place; in some instances this is not difficult to determine because familiar vocabulary and concepts point very clearly to specific lines of influence. What is not so easy to establish—and here scholarly consensus often breaks down—is the depth or significance of that influence. To use a concrete example, there is general agreement that Philo appropriated the language of Greek mystery religions. But how do we assess this fact? Where within the context of Philo's thought should we place this observation? Goodenough argued that Philo's mystical language ought to be taken at face value, for it signaled the existence of a literal mystery in Hellenistic Judaism.[17] Wolfson, on the other hand, assessed Philo's language in a completely different light. To him, if Alexandrian Jewish writers

> ever happen to use the terminology of the mysteries in their presentation of Jewish rites, it is either for the purpose of emphasizing the contrast between the religion of the Jews and the mysteries of the heathen, or because the terms derived from the mysteries have become part of the common speech and are used in a sense completely divorced from their original meaning.[18]

In other words there may be agreement about the "fact" of appropriation, but disagreement about its import and meaning.

The same problem arises regarding the liberal arts and sciences in Philo. (For the time being we may simply list these liberal disciplines—namely, grammar, rhetoric, dialectic, geometry, arithmetic, music, and astronomy.) One need only glance at Philo's treatise *De Congressu* to establish the fact that Philo appropriated the encyclical studies. But was he simply paying lip service to a Greek idea of education? Or did he take the encyclia more seriously? The chapters which follow address themselves to these questions.

The liberal arts and sciences provide a particularly fruitful field of study because of two anomalies, the first religious and the other philosophical. The religious anomaly appears when we reflect that even in modern times there is tension between the holy and the profane in the encounter of traditional religion and secular education. From the perspective of traditional religion, secular education has the taint of *this* world. What is more, secular education represents a threat to those steeped in religious tradition because it may bring in its wake a dilution of that tradition.

We may see an instance of this tension in the encounter of rabbinic Judaism with Greek Wisdom, or *hokhmah yewanit*.[19] First of all, it should be emphasized that Greek was actively studied in Palestine.[20] In the second century C.E., an academy was established in the House of the Patriarch, Rabban Gamliel. Concerning it, Rabbi Simeon, the son of the Patriarch, said: "There were a thousand young men in my father's house, five hundred of whom studied the Law, while the other five hundred studied Greek Wisdom" (*Sotah* 49b).[21] Although it could be argued that a dispensation was given to the House of the Patriarch because of its responsibility for dealing with the secular authorities of Rome, according to Lieberman there were other grounds for learning Greek. If a man wanted to teach his son the language as the basis for a future profession, he could do so, just as he was permitted to teach him any trade.[22] The study of astronomy and mathematics, while in some sense representative of alien wisdom, was actively encouraged. Doubtless because of their applicability to matters of Law, anyone able to learn these subjects "was obliged to do so."[23]

From the guidelines for the study of Greek set forth by Lieberman as well as from the well-known receptivity of the rabbis toward certain secular studies, it would appear that rabbinic interest in Greek learning was primarily utilitarian.[24] Two other Talmudic passages, in which the rabbis' distrust of Greek Wisdom is manifest, seem to reinforce this conclusion. In the first, the main fear of the authorities seems to be that if a child is too strongly impressed with an alien cultural ideal, he might grow up to be unreliable in his allegiance to his people.

> When the kings of the Hasmonean house fought one another, Hyrcanus was outside and Aristobulus within. Each day they used to let down *denarii* in a basket, and haul up for them [animals for] the continual offerings. An old man there, who was learned in Greek wisdom, spoke with them in Greek, saying, "As long as they carry on the Temple-service, they will never surrender to you." On the morrow they let down *denarii* in a basket, and hauled up a pig. When it reached half way up the wall, it stuck its claws into the wall and the land of Israel was shaken over a distance of four hundred parasangs. At that time they declared, "Cursed be a man who rears pigs and cursed be a man who teaches his son Greek Wisdom!" (*Sotah* 49b).[25]

The fact that this story grew out of the period of civil war between Hyrcanus II and Aristobulus II in 65 B.C.E.[26] might help to explain why Greek Wisdom appears here both as alien and threatening. More difficult to explain is another passage, in which the potential student of Greek Wisdom is Ben Damah, a man advanced in years and in the learning of Torah. Ben Damah asked R. Ishmael: "May one such as I who have studied the whole Torah learn Greek Wisdom?" R. Ishmael replied by citing a verse from the book of Joshua:

> "This book of the law shall not depart out of thy mouth, but thou shalt meditate therein day and night" (Josh. I, 8). Go then and find a time that is neither day nor night and learn then Greek Wisdom (*Menaḥoth* 99b).[27]

In this case, the student was not at a formative stage of his development. Nor was his request made within a context of social unrest. Why, then, was Ben Damah forbidden to study Greek Wisdom?

The most persuasive answer to this problem is given by Hallewy,[28] who points out that R. Ishmael's ruling appears in the Babylonian, not the Palestinian Talmud. In Palestine, Hellenism already was a part of the cultural life of a sector of the Jewish population. Although the language was often acquired merely to enhance social status,[29] the rabbis of Palestine admitted that certain truths existed among the gentiles, and they did not want the Jews to be the only people in the Hellenistic world who were ignorant of those truths.[30]

In Babylon, however, Greek was not part of the life of the people. The entire question of Greek Wisdom was a theoretical one there and, for this reason, the Talmudic authorities could afford to be very severe. Hence the strictness of the passage from *Menaḥoth*. Ben Damah is not merely asking whether the ban on the teaching of Greek Wisdom extends to self-instruction.[31] Rather, Ben Damah already knows that it is forbidden to study as well as to teach things Greek. The purpose of the question, in Hallewy's opinion, is to test the rationale given by the rabbis. That is, does the argument that the study of Greek Wisdom causes one to neglect the Torah weigh against someone who is learned in the Scriptures? The answer is uncompromising and in the affirmative. The ban on Greek Wisdom is total—applying, as far as the Babylonian rabbinical authorities were concerned, even to men who, by hypothesis, were well advanced in age and religious learning.[32]

In both Palestine and Babylonia the authorities were cognizant of the closeness of Greek Wisdom to heresy. Within each context, they did what they could to prevent Jewish children from growing up with "Greek souls."[33] They were aware that the study of Greek Wisdom could be beneficial, even to a Jew living within the Talmudic tradition. There was, after all, an advantage in being able to deal effectively with secular rulers or scholars from other peoples. A discipline such as astronomy or mathematics might also aid the faithful in the observance of the Torah.[34] Nevertheless the rabbis exhibited caution and distrust toward the Wisdom of Greece. To the extent that the Palestinian authorities were receptive to Greek Wisdom,[35] they were simply allowing what they could not effectively prohibit.

The rabbinic reception of Greek Wisdom may be seen as a prototypical response by traditional religious authorities to a secular body of information. In times of turmoil, mistrust and fear come to the surface. At other times, controlled access to secular information is allowed. At best Greek Wisdom may be useful; at worst it is dangerous. But no passages indicate that Greek Wisdom should be esteemed for its inherent value. Now I do not wish to compare this rabbinic response to Philo's view of secular education. There are too many variables and unknowns. Philo was one Jewish individual living in a Greek world; the rabbis were in positions of legal and moral authority. But both the rabbis and Philo must have confronted the same problem: how does one reconcile a secular body of information, which would seem to have no inherent spiritual value, with the holy teachings of Scripture? Nothing in the basic core of Philo's beliefs gave him an easy answer to this question. Yet his view of the nature of man and man's duty to God, especially his view of ordinary men and the goals to which they could aspire, led him to reconcile the religious anomalies presented by secular education. As we shall see, Philo's reconciliation had implications for his conception of mankind and for his theology.

The second anomaly is philosophical. In order to appreciate it fully, it is necessary to understand the metaphysical and pedagogical position which the encyclia were traditionally assigned. According to an ancient maxim attributed to Ariston of Chios, "Those who neglect philosophy and spend their time on ordinary studies are like the Suitors who desired Penelope but slept with her maids."[36] For more than one writer in antiquity this analogy expressed the subordination of the liberal arts and sciences to philosophy. Just as the maids were unworthy replacements for Penelope, so the liberal disciplines, which constituted the core of nonphilosophical training in the ancient world, were poor substitutes for philosophy. Proponents of this view maintained that the liberal arts and sciences should not be studied in their own right, but only as preliminary studies to the higher knowledge of philosophy.

The view attributed to Ariston, that the encyclia should be propaedeutic in nature, is in keeping with the subordinate status given to the liberal disciplines from Xenophon to Seneca.[37] Perhaps the most influential philosopher to relegate the encyclia to such a position was Plato. In Book vii of the *Republic* Glaucon and Socrates agree that a potential guardian should first familiarize himself with arithmetic, plane and solid geometry, astronomy, and music. For, as Socrates says of arithmetic, "it is one of those studies which we are seeking that naturally conduce to the awakening of thought . . ." (523a). In the same spirit, Socrates suggests that geometry facilitates "the conversion of the soul itself from the world of generation to essence and truth" (525c). In Plato, these studies lead to the contemplation of "what is best among realities" (532c).[38]

The very disciplines which Plato discusses in the *Republic*—arithmetic, geometry, astronomy, and music—reappear in post-classical times as the *quadrivium*. Taken together with the literary arts of grammar, rhetoric, and dialectic (the *trivium*), they comprise the encyclia (*enkyklios paideia*). Although the technical term *enkyklios paideia* is not attested earlier than in the works of Diodorus Siculus and Dionysius of Halicarnassus in the latter part of the first century B.C.E.,[39] the *quadrivium* already provided the cornerstone for Plato's educational theories and are considered together or in part by subsequent classical and Hellenistic authors, including Philo of Alexandria.

In Philo's work *De Congressu,* the Penelope-analogy appears in a slightly altered form. Penelope is transformed into Sarah, the first Jewish matriarch, and the maids are identified with Hagar. Because the terms of the maxim are so familiar, it has generally been assumed that Philo's conception of the role of the encyclia was the same as that of his predecessors. In this monograph I shall argue that this assumption is inadequate. For if Philo had adopted the view that secular education had value solely as a propaedeutic to higher learning, this already would have been a major concession from a man of deep religious convictions. But Philo goes further than the traditional view of the liberal arts and sciences as stepping-stones to philosophy. He endows the encyclia with inherent spiritual value; this position represents a significant shift in the history of liberal studies.

The fact that Philo appropriates the encyclia at all is an anomaly. It is easy to understand how Philo might be able to appropriate (with suitable modifications) the higher reaches of Greek philosophy. The appeal of this material to a man of the Hellenistic age who sought spiritual truth is self-evident. What is remarkable about Philo's seizing on the encyclia is that when all is said and done they are simply extensions of the mundane world. This is why Plato, in his ideal educational scheme, could not endow them with greater significance. Yet despite Philo's allegiance to Plato, Philo did not hesitate to appropriate the liberal disciplines. In fact he went one step further, incorporating them in his theology.

On the issue of secular education, Philo may be viewed as moving against the current of his times. From both a religious and a philosophical point of view, Philo confounds our expectations. It is tempting to regard this situation as an expression of Philo's eclectic or even his idiosyncratic nature. When we reflect, however, that Philo must have seen education as a key to Jewish survival in Alexandria, it becomes impossible simply to dismiss Philo's treatment of secular thought, for his views on that subject are a fitting measure of the extent of his accommodation to the alien culture which surrounded him.

Works abound on Philo's own education—that is, analyses of the subject matters and sources to which he must have been exposed. But only Colson,[40] Marcus,[41] and Alexandre[42] have addressed themselves specifically to Philo's system of secular education and the encyclical studies. My study differs from theirs insofar as it draws out the social, philosophical, and theological implications of Philo's position. *De Congressu* contains the most extended remarks on education, but neither there nor elsewhere in the Philonic corpus is an exhaustive study of education the exclusive aim. At no time does Philo devote himself single-mindedly to the topic of education as he does, for instance, to the proposition that every good man is free (in *Quod Omnis Probus Liber sit*). *De Congressu* is part of a larger whole, the *Allegory,* in which Philo's first allegiance is to the Biblical text. While he is ingenious at bending his interpretations to his concerns, *De Congressu* is still unavoidably shaped by the first verses in Genesis 16. Moreover, we shall be obliged to cite treatises which are even less directly concerned with education than *De Congressu* is. The fact that issues bearing on the encyclia often appear in seemingly irrelevant contexts is troublesome, but reflects a state of affairs with which every student of Philo must contend.[43]

In order to achieve the greatest degree of clarity at the least expense to Philo's inimitable patterns of thought, I cite other ancient authors relatively rarely. For the question of secular education in Philo is linked to and is an expression of Jewish accommodation to the pagan world. If we proceed from that assumption, then the confluence of ideas which surrounds this issue is unique to Philo. To be sure, other ancient writers were concerned with the question of secular education. But Philo, a Jew who sought to reconcile the tensions of two cultures, was alone in responding to the issue as a theological and cultural challenge. For this reason, I shall allow Philo to speak in his own voice, unmediated by predecessors and successors.

Chapter 1

Encyclical Studies in Philo

1. Terminology

Socrates states in the *Gorgias* that he cannot determine whether a man is happy until he knows how the man stands with respect to *paideia* and justice (470e 6). To understand this use of the term *paideia*, we must distinguish two meanings which the word had in antiquity. One sense of *paideia* is the process of education whereby a child was equipped to take his place in adult society. The second is the end result of that instruction, the state of the completely cultivated human being.[1] The two meanings are related as the means and the end: *paideia* in the sense of the cultivated mind is the result and purpose of *paideia* in its educational meaning. And whereas the process of *paideia* comes to an end with adolescence, the ideal of *paideia* continues to attract a man throughout his life. Plato evokes the second meaning of the term in the *Gorgias* passage. *Paideia* in this sense has a long history, for it represents a cultural ideal which animated the classical world.[2]

Although Philo used *paideia* in senses related to the process of education, he also clearly understood the term as the end result of instruction.[3] For instance, he praises the accomplishments in *paideia* of non-Jews who were magnanimous toward his people (*Leg.* 245, 320). In one passage, he links *paideia* and virtue, noting that for their sake "no war either foreign or civil has ever yet broken out; for these things are by nature peaceful; and when they prevail, a settled condition of society, and the reign of law, and all things fairest to behold, meet . . ." (*Post.* 118). Love of *paideia* is given as one of the motivations for men traveling abroad (*Abr.* 65). Elsewhere, in referring to the fruit of *paideia*, Philo says it

> . . . . shall be, subsist, remain free from interference, through all the divisions of time. This is equivalent to saying that throughout eternity it is exempt from corruption; for the nature of good is incorruptible (*Plant.* 114).

Just as *paideia* is valued for its civilizing qualities, "its absence (*apaideusia*) is the cause of disease and destruction" (*Ebr.* 141). In the same spirit, Philo says that "it is against the untrained (*anagōgōn*) and undisciplined (*apaideutōn*) more perhaps than against any other person that the lawgiver breathes slaughter" (*Ebr.* 13). Accordingly, Philo regards those people who have not been exposed to *paideia* as uncivilized (*barbaroi, Spec.* iii.163). The term "unclean" in another passage is itself sufficient to raise the spectre of inadequate preparation in *paideia*:

1

> By unclean (*mē katharous*) I mean all those who without ever tasting educa-tion (*paideias*) at all, or else having received it in a crooked and distorted form, have changed the stamp of wisdom's beauty into the ugliness of sophistry (*Prob.* 4).

It is no wonder that Philo describes Cain's city as lacking in *paideia* and plagued by numerous evils as well:

> His [Cain's] inhabitants are the wise in their own conceit, devotees of impiety, godlessness, self-love, arrogance, false opinion, men ignorant of real wisdom, who have reduced to an organized system ignorance, lack of learning and of culture (*agnoian kai apaideusian kai amathian*), and other pestilential things akin to these (*Post.* 52).

The personal quest for *paideia* was a serious and rewarding experience for men. Its acquisition was a life-long concern, befitting man's maturity no less than the days of his youth. As Philo writes in *De Somniis*:

> There is a story that a grey-haired man of great age shed tears when dying, not in any cowardly fear of death, but by reason of his yearning for educa-tion (*paideias himeron*), and the thought that he is now first entering upon it, when he takes his final leave of it (*Som.* i.10).

Philo states that he himself possessed this desire. After describing the "ocean of civil cares" in which he was often immersed, he says:

> Yet amid my groans I hold my own, for, planted in my soul from my ear-liest days I keep the yearning for culture (*paideias himeron*) which ever has pity and compassion for me . . . (*Spec.* iii.4).

These passages, which involve the fully developed minds of men, are sufficient to place Philo among the Hellenistic proponents of *paideia* as a cultural ideal.[4]

Enkyklios paideia in Philo refers specifically to education in the liberal arts and sciences. We might say, subject to later qualification, that these disciplines contribute to the overall development of *paideia* by providing the cornerstone on which philosophical culture is built.[5] A more precise understanding of *enkyklios paideia* requires a closer look at that term. The most obvious survival of *enkyklios paideia* in modern languages is the word "encyclopedia."[6] But despite the modern use of "encyclopedia" to refer to the totality of human knowledge,[7] *enkyklios paideia* had no such reference in antiquity.

Until recently, in accordance with the Hellenistic Greek meaning of *en-kyklios,* the term *enkyklios paideia* was taken to mean "the usual everyday educa-tion received by all."[8] This interpretation has been challenged by Alexandre[9] and de Rijk,[10] both of whom take issue with the attribution of ordinary mean-ings to the term *enkyklios.*

In de Rijk's view, in order to ascertain what *enkyklios paideia* originally meant as a technical (educational) term, it is necessary to take into account the earliest evidence for the meaning of *enkyklios,* not merely Hellenistic usage. Since *enkyklios* seems to have been an equivalent of *choreios* or *chorikos* as early as the first half of the fifth century B.C.E.,[11] de Rijk argues that the term originally related to musical terminology.[12] It acquired a broader educational sense by virtue of the harmony which both music and general culture were supposed to instill in a man.

De Rijk's analysis is particularly relevant because the classical connection between *enkyklios* and musical terminology appears later in Philo. As a good number of passages indicate,[13] this association of ideas was clearly fixed in Philo's mind. On the basis of this evidence, we may tentatively suggest that Philo thought of *enkyklios paideia* not as ordinary, everyday training, but as education in harmony. In the ensuing pages, we shall substantiate this suggestion and elaborate on it from several different points of view.

In addition to the standard term *enkyklios paideia,* Philo uses various synonymous expressions to denote the encyclical studies.[14] The adjective *mesos* appears in three of these: namely, *mesē paideia, mesai epistēmai,* and *mesai technai.*[15] The fact that *mesos* recurs would seem to warrant further investigation. According to Colson,

> In strict Stoic usage *mesa = adiaphora, i.e.* things which are neither good nor bad. Still sometimes the word seems to acquire the rather different force of things midway between good and bad and therefore having a definite value, though not the highest.[16]

A study of Philo's use of the word *mesos* in contexts unrelated to secular education confirms the fact that Philo often ascribes to *mesos* a definite value.[17] On the basis of Philo's general usage, we can accept Colson's conclusion that the connotation of the term *mesē paideia* is not neutral.

Several final observations on terminology are in order. The word *technē,* as Marrou points out, had an ancient tie with the liberal arts.[18] *Technai* in Philo may denote various arts, such as that of the painter, the sculptor, the performer, or the charioteer. The term is also used in reference to the craft of the hunter, the builder, or Nature herself in fashioning human form (the latter in *Spec.* i.266). In view of the wide diversity of these uses, it is no wonder that Philo should introduce modifiers when *technē* refers specifically to the encyclia. Thus *mesai technai* in *Cong.* 143–44 clearly denotes the encyclical disciplines, as does *theōrētikai technai* in *LA* i.57:

> For some of the arts and sciences are theoretical (*theōrētikai*) indeed but not practical (*praktikai*), such as geometry and astronomy, and some are practical, but not theoretical, as the arts of the carpenter and coppersmith, and all that are called mechanical (*banausoi*).

In this passage, Philo distinguishes between two classes of *technai*.[19] Obviously, the general term may be used to encompass arts which have little in common with the encyclia. Yet we also find instances of Philo's using the word *technai* without modifiers to refer to encyclical studies.

> We give the name of arts (*technas*) therefore to music, grammar and the kindred arts, and accordingly those who by means of them reach fulness of accomplishment are called artists (*technitai*), whether they are musicians or grammarians (*Cong.* 142).

There is an ambiguity, then, over whether *technai* is to be understood in the narrow sense of "encyclia" or in a broader sense which would include other crafts.[20] In our study, however, it is sufficient to recall that even when *technai* does not have a clear encyclical connotation, Philo's reflections on the *technai* often are generalizations based on his understanding of the liberal disciplines or, alternatively, are directly applicable to them.

2. The Individual Disciplines

Like his contemporaries, Philo had a distinct set of disciplines in mind when referring to the encyclia. We may demonstrate this by working, as it were, backwards. By the Middle Ages, seven liberal arts and sciences were clearly recognized.[21] They were divided into two groups—the *trivium,* which was composed of grammar, rhetoric, and dialectic, and the *quadrivium,* which was composed of geometry, arithmetic, music, and astronomy. With this group of disciplines in view, let us turn to Philo's treatises. We first learn that in one context or another Philo mentions all these studies. What is more important, as Kühnert notes, Philo never mentions other studies (e.g., medicine) in those passages which refer to the encyclia.[22]

At the same time, despite numerous references to secular education in his works and a treatise largely devoted to the subject, Philo never gives a definitive enumeration of the disciplines which he included in the encyclia. In explanation, Alexandre has suggested that Philo had a "repugnance for exhaustive accounts."[23] He also may have assumed that his contemporaries were familiar with the studies and were in no need of a definitive list.

The most effective way to study the individual disciplines is to concentrate on those passages in which three or more of the studies are mentioned in a context which is related to education.[24] By this criterion, we arrive at eight significant enumerations of the encyclia in Philo: *Cong.* 74–77; *Cher.* 105; *Agr.* 18; *Som.* i.205; *QE* ii.103; *Cong.* 11, 15–18; *QG* iii.21; and *Mos.* i.23.

The last-mentioned passage is one of the more interesting and controversial.[25] Philo says in *Mos.* i.21 that teachers came to instruct Moses "some unbidden from the neighbouring countries and the provinces of Egypt, others only portray instances of human frailty and provide negative examples for our "instruction."

Philo is just as aware of the limits of grammar as he is of its purpose. *Cong.* 149–50 makes this clear:

> When therefore they discourse on the parts of speech, are they not encroaching on, and casually appropriating the discoveries of philosophy? For it is the exclusive property of philosophy to examine what a conjunction is, or a noun, or a verb, or a common as distinguished from a proper noun. . . . For to her is due the system which embraces the study of complete sentences and propositions and predicates.[39]

Grammar thus ends when the inquiry turns to what elements of the discipline really *are*. If a student followed this course of study upward he would find himself making philosophical distinctions. Nevertheless, one had to beware: both poetry and music had charms which could beguile the student's sense of hearing, disorient his soul, and weaken his resistance to idolatry.[40]

Rhetoric. In the eight enumerations of the encyclical studies, rhetoric appears five times.[41] Since rhetoric is a skill to be developed rather than a substantive body of knowledge to be learned, it is not surprising that Philo gives us no indication of the specific subject matter to be covered.[42] Instead, in *De Somniis* i.205, there is a list of the powers which the student of rhetoric (*rhētorikē*) sought to cultivate: "conception, expression, arrangement, treatment, memory, delivery" (*heuresin, phrasin, taxin, oikonomian, mnēmēn, hypokrisin*). These are "fundamental divisions of rhetoric which appear in the same form in most of the rhetorical treatises."[43]

Rhetoric, Philo says, "will make the man a true master of words and thoughts" (*Cong.* 17). The question which this statement poses is why such a mastery should be important to Philo.[44] The answer may be found in *Det.* 34–42. In that passage, virtuous men, such as Abel and Moses, find themselves in situations where verbal ability becomes a matter of vital importance. "Abel has never learned arts of speech (*technas . . . logōn*), and knows the beautiful and noble with his mind only" (*Det.* 37). Because Abel was not equipped to speak, Cain did not find it difficult to "gain the mastery over him by plausible sophistries" (*Det.* 1). Moses, on the other hand, wisely let his brother Aaron speak for him.

The advantage which Aaron had and Abel lacked was skill in rhetoric. In Philo's view, skill in this discipline had a particular urgency; it was an essential weapon in the battle against Alexandrian sophists of whom, if we are to believe Philo, there were many:

> When we have been exercised in the forms which words take (*tas tōn logōn ideas*), we shall no more sink to the ground through inexperience of the

tricks of the sophistic wrestling, but we shall spring up and carry on the
struggle and disentangle ourselves with ease from the grips which their art
has taught them (*Det.* 41).[45]

Rhetoric functions, then, in a defensive way, protecting the virtuous and the
inarticulate from sophistic attacks.

The primary goal of rhetoric, however, was not simply to develop superficial skills which any "clever wrestler" might acquire. Rather, its central goal
was to insure that speech *interpreted* thought properly. What Philo meant by
this has been discussed at length by several modern commentators.[46] In brief,
Philo adopted the Stoic position that *logos* could be divided in two parts:
"reason which suggests the ideas with clearness, and the speech which gives
unfailing expression to them" (*Mig.* 73).[47] Because of this division, "many
reason excellently, but find speech a bad interpreter of thought and are by it
betrayed, through not having had a thorough grounding in the ordinary subjects of culture" (*mousikēn tēn enkyklion ouk ekponēsantes, Mig.* 72). As indicated by
the last phrase, the encyclia enter at this point and are responsible for facilitat-
ing the movement from reason or thought which is within the mind (*logos
endiathetos*) to *logos* which is projected in speech (*logos prophorikos*).

As a skill to be mastered rather than a specific body of knowledge, rhetoric
does not reach a point at which the discipline "becomes" philosophy. Put
another way, philosophy, whose province is the definition of key terms, does
not have a particular role to play in the advanced study of rhetoric. This does
not mean that rhetoric is unaffected by higher considerations. The student of
rhetoric must always stay within the framework of religious truth and virtue.
For without those guidelines, the same art which is used in the defense of truth
may be turned into a weapon against it.

Those who practice rhetoric with no concern for truth fit the classical definition of the sophist. Philo characterizes the *sophistēs* (taken in its pejorative
sense)[48] as having a "love of arguing for arguing's sake. This character aims its
shafts at all representatives of the sciences (*mathēmatōn*), opposing each indi-
vidually and all in common . . ." (*Fug.* 209–10).[49] The sophist for Philo is also
one whose education in rhetoric has misfired. Sophists may, in fact, have wide
learning,[50] but, resolved to "contradict all men" (*QG* iii.33), they distort their
disciplines. By the destructive power of sophistry, a discipline may be turned
into a non-discipline. As Philo says in *LA* iii.36:

> For thou fanciest thyself one versed in science because thou hast conned
> over methods of persuasion unworthy of an educated man, wherewith to
> combat the truth. But thy science proves itself no science. . . .

It is no accident, then, that sophistry is epitomized by Ishmael, who is portrayed as the misbegotten child of Abraham's apprenticeship to the encyclia.[51]
Since sophistry is often depicted as the result of miseducation in rhetoric, it

would be instructive to discuss other characteristics which Philo attributes to the sophists. For by seeing the negative aspects of the sophistic life, we might learn what a man stands to gain by proper training in the encyclical discipline of rhetoric. One distinguishing mark of Philonic sophistry is its petty contentiousness. In *Cong.* 53, sophists, who are seen as practicing a negative sort of philosophy,[52] are reduced to battling over syllables.

> And so too in philosophy there are men who are merely word-mongers and word-hunters (*logopōlai kai logothērai*), who neither wish nor practise to cure their life, brimful of infirmities as it is, but from their earliest years to extreme old age contend in battles of argument (*gnōsimachountes*)[53] and battles of syllables and blush not to do so. They act as though happiness depended on the endless fruitless hypercriticism (*periergia*) of words as such (*onomatōn kai rhēmatōn*), instead of on establishing on a better basis character, the fount of human life . . .

Philo touches on the same theme in *Agr.* 136:

> Day after day the swarm of sophists to be found everywhere wears out the ears of any audience they happen to have with disquisitions on minutiae, unravelling phrases that are ambiguous and can bear two meanings. . . .

This particular penchant of sophists for quibbling and maximizing ambiguity can be traced back to rhetoric where, in a less destructive form, such techniques might function legitimately as methods of persuasion in the service of truth. As sophistic devices, however, these techniques may be applied by misguided specialists to each of the encyclical disciplines for the sole purpose of splitting hairs.[54]

Another characteristic of the sophist mentioned in *Cong.* 53 is that he makes no attempt to "cure" his life.[55] To cure one's life it is necessary to *act* on the belief that "true philosophy . . . is woven from three strands—thoughts, words and deeds—united into a single piece for the attainment and enjoyment of happiness" (*Mos.* ii.212).[56] Absorbed in argument for its own sake or for mercenary reasons,[57] the sophist is constitutionally incapable of joining theory and practice. His life is irreconcilably divided:

> The words of these [sophists] deserve praise, but their lives censure, for they are capable of saying the best, but incapable of doing it (*Cong.* 67).

Cleft in two, the sophist is reduced to imagining that "wisdom consists in finding specious arguments, and not in appealing to the solid evidence of facts (*pragmatōn, Mig.* 171).

Central to Philo's conception of sophistic miseducation is the fact that those who have succumbed to its temptations float, free from all moorings, amid various philosophies. Just as there are sophists "who declare the universe to be uncreated," there are also sophists who "maintain its creation" (*Heres* 246). For Philo the correctness of the latter position is obvious. Yet a sophist is not redeemed simply because he happens upon the view that the world is created; he still lacks a faith that truth exists. Such a faith is essential to the very act of searching in a meaningful way. Thus Philo criticizes sophists who "place no foundation under their opinions and doctrines and do not (prefer) one thing to another . . ." (*QG* iii.33). For without some "foundation" on the basis of which preferences among opinions can be formed, human endeavor is vain.[58]

The sophists' disregard for the truth is not limited to practical affairs. Sooner or later, they extend "the activities of their word-cleverness to heaven itself" (*Som.* ii.283). Herein lie two sorts of heresy. First, there are substantive heresies. As a sophist, one is called upon to adopt *any* view which is, at the moment, expedient. Even though the sophist does not possess the requisite virtue to discourse on divine matters, his vocation does not permit him to shrink from them. Indeed, Philo pictures the sophist tackling lofty subjects with the same bravado that marks the latter's other encounters. Unaware of the implications of flights heavenward, sophists mindlessly adopt heretical views. The second sort of heresy incurred by sophists is based on their presumptions, rather than on the substantive doctrines they might adopt. Now Philo asserts that in their misguided craft, sophists rely entirely on speech. Their dependence on this faculty is suspect because in Philo speech is intended as an instrument of thought, not as a substitute for it.[59]

Dialectic. Dialectic is one of the more problematic encyclia in Philo. First of all, in the eight enumerations, dialectic is mentioned only once—in *Cong.* 18. This reference should be cited in full:

> Dialectic (*dialektikē*), the sister and twin, as some have said, of Rhetoric, distinguishes true argument from false, and convicts the plausibilities of sophistry, and thus will heal that great plague of the soul, deceit.

In her discussion of dialectic, Alexandre speaks of the "ambivalent nature" of the discipline.[60] Philo himself is at least partly responsible for the ambivalence. By calling dialectic and rhetoric twin sisters, he stresses what the disciplines have in common,[61] not what distinguishes them. Of course dialectic and rhetoric share several elements.[62] For instance, in Philo neither has a specific subject matter. Likewise, they are united by a common purpose: to marshal arguments against sophistry.

At the same time, dialectic and rhetoric differ. One ancient author who addressed himself to this issue in a more rigorous way than Philo did was Diogenes Laertius.[63] In the following passage, Diogenes attributes certain distinctions to Zeno of Citium which Philo would have found congenial:

> Further, by rhetoric they [the Stoics] understand the science of speaking

well on matters set forth by plain narrative, and by dialectic that of correctly discussing subjects by question and answer; hence their alternative definition of it as the science of statements true, false, and neither true nor false (vii.42).[64]

We may see from this passage that the emphasis in rhetoric is on speaking well, not on formal technicalities. In his discussion of rhetoric, Philo does not make specific reference to truth or falsity—and with good reason. In verbal wrestling, one hold is as good as another; in combat with a sophist, one may even use sophistic devices just so long as one does not become a sophist in the process.

Dialectic, unlike rhetoric, is a structured discipline which is designed to discover truth and falsity by probing into the particulars of the argument. The more formal aspects of dialectic may be seen in *Agr.* 13; here Philo says that dialectic whets the mind, "compelling it to pay keen attention to each problem as it presents itself; and enabling it to draw clear distinctions, and to make the special character of the matter in hand stand out in bold relief against the background of the features which it has in common with others."

The structured aspect of dialectic has led more than one commentator to compare dialectic with logic which, strictly speaking, is one of the three parts of Stoic philosophy.[65] In comparing dialectic with logic, we should not lose sight of the fact that we are dealing with two distinct levels. Dialectic, like the other encyclical disciplines, grows out of real-life situations or concrete observations. Philosophy is a more abstract, higher mode of thought.[66] Nevertheless, despite fundamental differences, it is instructive to take note of Philo's analysis of logic. Logic, we learn in *Agr.* 16,

> disentangles ambiguous expressions capable of two meanings, and exposes the fallacies created by tricks of argument, and using perfectly clear and unmistakable language and adducing proofs which admit of no doubt destroys plausible falsehood, that greatest snare and pest of the soul . . .

Logic, then, is a well-honed instrument for abstract analysis. Dialectic, by contrast, is a more practical discipline; it is used in discussion to oppose concrete errors. For instance, one would resort to dialectic as the appropriate literary art to defend the doctrinal points made in *Opif.* 170–72. For such an elevated purpose, rhetoric would not be suitable. For if rhetoric may be compared to struggles waged in the wrestling pits, dialectic should be compared to confrontations occurring in the halls of the academy.

Geometry. Geometry, the first of the four mathematical branches of the encyclia to be considered, is the only discipline mentioned in all eight enumerations. Perhaps geometry is mentioned frequently because in antiquity *geōmetria* had an expanded, as well as a narrow, meaning. That is, it could be used in a general sense to refer to disciplines other than pure geometry as we know it.[67] In Philo, the term seems to be linked particularly with arithmetic. Nevertheless, our analysis will treat these disciplines separately.

Two distinct reasons for studying geometry are given by Philo. The first (which likewise applies to the study of arithmetic) is practical: to produce "absolute accuracy in matters which require a making of calculations and noting of proportion" (*Som.* i.205). The second is basically moral:

> Geometry (*geōmetria*) will sow in the soul that loves to learn the seeds of equality (*isotētos*) and proportion (*analogias*), and by the charm of its logical continuity will raise from those seeds a zeal for justice (*dikaiosynēs, Cong.* 16).

The belief that geometrical studies will produce equality and proportion also appears in *Cher.* 105 and *Cong.* 75.

Philo thus places considerable emphasis on equality, both as the major characteristic of the discipline per se and as a desirable lesson to be gained from its study. What, we might ask, is Philo's particular interest in equality? Goodenough supplies us with a plausible explanation. According to him, Philo uses *isotēs* "as one of the chief principles in the cosmos, if not the fundamental one."[68] Since *isotēs* grows exclusively out of a familiarity with geometry, the centrality of that discipline becomes clear. The position of geometry is further underscored by Philo's assigning geometric figures to the four elements which constitute the material world.[69]

Before turning to arithmetic, we should note the limits of geometry. As in the case of grammar, Philo indicates the point at which the encyclical study of geometry becomes philosophy:

> Such . . . matters as isosceles and scalene triangles, and circles and polygons and the other figures are the discovery of geometry; but when we come to the nature of the point, the line, the superficies and the solid which are the roots and foundations (*rhizai kai themelioi*) of those named above, we leave geometry behind. For whence does she obtain the definition of a point as that which has no parts, of a line as length without breadth, of superficies as that which has length and breadth only, and of a solid as that which has three dimensions, length, breadth, and depth? For these belong to philosophy . . . (*Cong.* 146–47).[70]

Arithmetic. Four enumerations of the encyclia mention this discipline. Since two of the passages do not survive in Greek (*QE* ii.103 and *QG* iii.21), the term Philo employed there is lost. In *Mos.* i.23, *arithmos* refers to the encyclical study even though, in the majority of its uses elsewhere in Philo, this word has no such technical meaning. The term *arithmētikē* appears in the fourth enumeration, *Som.* i.205. This passage, already noted in connection with geometry, states the purpose of studying arithmetic; it is to attain "absolute accuracy in matters which require a making of calculations and noting of proportion."

As we have seen, Philo tended to use geometry in ways which would strike a modern student of the subject as fanciful (e.g., assigning geometric figures to the four elements). This tendency is even more pronounced in Philo's use of arithmetic. The study of arithmetic involved learning numerological lore which for Philo was often a key to problems arising from Scripture. Why, for instance, did Moses allow men to eat exactly ten graminivorous animals? Philo explains, relying on numerological lore:

> For as he [Moses] always adhered to the principles of numerical science (*tēs arithmētikēs theōrias*), which he knew by close observance to be a paramount factor in all that exists, he never enacted any law great or small without calling to his aid and as it were accommodating to his enactment its appropriate (*oikeion*) number. But of all the numbers from the unit upwards ten is the most perfect, and, as Moses says, most holy and sacred (*Spec.* iv.105).

Before proceeding, we should make one observation: numerological lore for Philo was part and parcel of arithmetic. Marrou could just as well have been thinking of Philo when he wrote of the ancient Greeks in general that they "never managed to disentangle their ideas about numbers from . . . qualitative elements."[71] In view of this situation, how do we determine the limits of the encyclical discipline of arithmetic?

Students of ancient mathematics have met this difficulty by introducing a distinction between arithmetic and arithmology. The latter has been defined as "that genre of remarks on the formation, the value and the importance of the ten first numbers, in which sound scientific research and the fantasies of religion and philosophy mingle."[72] With this definition in mind, Robbins is able to separate the arithmetical wheat from the chaff in Philo. When the former is recovered,

> There will be found to be a residue of material, however, that is more properly classed with what is *now* called "arithmology," which is wholly Pythagorean and hardly scientific in any sense. In the analysis that follows, accordingly, a distinction will be made between Philo's arithmetic and his arithmology.[73]

For convenience, let us adopt the distinction made by Robbins. In so doing, however, we must bear clearly in mind that the difference between arithmetic and arithmology is an anachronism. Philo himself gives no indication, linguistic or otherwise, of being aware of it.

The scope of Philo's arithmetic, then, extends from passages in which the discipline seems to appear in a modern, "scientific" sense to passages of numerical lore. Robbins has explored the more rigorous "arithmetic" end of this continuum, concluding that Philo had some technical knowledge of the decimal system, classes of numbers, theorems concerning powers, proportions and the like.[74] Even at its best, this "arithmetic" knowledge does not rise to the level of sound scientific research. Technical passages in a strict sense are relatively rare.

Many passages dealing with numbers in Philo could be characterized as a mixture of non-technical arithmetic and lore.[75] One example will suffice:

> When, then, Moses says, "He finished His work on the sixth day," we must understand him to be adducing not a quantity of days, but a perfect number (*teleion arithmon*), namely six, since it is the first that is equal to the sum of its own fractions one-half, one-third, and one-sixth, and is produced by the multiplication of two unequal factors, 2 x 3; and see, the numbers 2 and 3 have left behind the incorporeal character that belongs to 1, 2 being an image of matter . . . while 3 is the image of a solid body . . . (*LA* i.3).

In passages such as these, we can find traces of arithmetic, for there are references to factors and fractions. Yet this "scientific" thread, which appears and reappears in Philo's works, is counter-balanced by the lore which Philo almost endlessly spins out.

Much of Philo's arithmetic must have involved associating numbers by "scientific" manipulations to certain moral values. Many of these passages do not betray even a trace of the "science" as we know it. For want of a better term we may call them "pure arithmology."[76] Here we reach the opposite end of the continuum:

> As for the number seven, the precedence awarded to it among all that exists is explained by the students of mathematics (*hoi peri ta mathēmata diatrip-santes*), who have investigated it with the utmost care and consideration. It is the virgin among the numbers, the essentially motherless, the closest bound to the initial Unit . . . (*Decal.* 102).

This, then, is the scope of the encyclical study as Philo actually used it for his own purposes and as he must have conceived of it for the training of the young.[77] Indeed, the place of arithmetic as part of Philonic secular education can hardly be overestimated, for the interpretation of all the numbers which appear in the Pentateuch depends directly upon it.[78]

Music. Music is mentioned in six of the eight enumerations given by Philo.[79] The most extensive reference is in *Cong.* 76:

> Again my ardour [for learning] moved me to keep company with a third;[80] rich in rhythm, harmony and melody was she, and her name was Music (*mousikē*), and from her I begat diatonics, chromatics and enharmonics,

conjunct and disjunct melodies, conforming with the consonance of the fourth, fifth or octave intervals.

Two important issues arise in this passage. First, as Alexandre points out, Philo is familiar with a technical musical vocabulary.[81] Secondly, this passage indicates the extent to which the encyclical study of music was oriented toward theory. In the latter respect, it is relevant that in *Opif.* 96 Philo refers to the study as *kanonikē theōria*.[82] In a brief glimpse at the music-master (*mousikos*) in *LA* iii.121, we again see the theoretical orientation of music.[83]

Considerations of a theoretical nature were at the forefront of the encyclical study of music. Or, to put it more precisely, the encyclia as an *ideal* curriculum would have emphasized the theoretical side of the discipline. There is no reason to suppose, however, that general education in music was limited strictly to theory.[84] Moses' own studies, as depicted by Philo, illustrate this point. In *Mos.* i.23, we learn that as a child Moses was taught "the whole subject of music as shown by the use of instruments (*dia chrēseōs organōn*) or in textbooks and treatises of a more special character."[85]

Other passages indicate that music included a non-theoretical side. For instance, in *Cher.* 105 Philo says that fine music heals "all that is harsh and inharmonious or discordant in the soul." In a passage which gives the virtues of several encyclical studies, Philo elaborates on this theme:

> Music will charm away the unrhythmic by its rhythm, the inharmonious by its harmony, the unmelodious and tuneless by its melody, and thus reduce discord to concord (*Cong.* 16).

Clearly Philo conceives of music as a discipline broad enough to include practical training which in turn has a practical effect. That effect could not be achieved by textbook study alone.

In thinking of music we should not be influenced by Philo's insistence that one must shun those arts which cater to pleasure.[86] Despite Philo's tendencies toward asceticism, music could have a positive communal function, for among the Therapeutae, rhythm, harmony, and melody were devoted to the service of God.[87]

Astronomy. It is appropriate that we should conclude our survey of the arts and sciences with astronomy. If students of the encyclia in antiquity followed any particular sequence of studies, astronomy would have been last, for its province is "the fairest and most exact of material things" (Plato, *Rep.* 529d).[88] As queen of the sciences, astronomy "compels the soul to look upward and leads it away from things here to those higher things" (*ibid.* 529a). Philo seems to have concurred with these views. Abraham, Philo's exemplary student of the encyclia, moved from astronomy directly to the higher reaches of the spirit.

The study of astronomy is mentioned only once in Philo's eight enumerations of the encyclia—in *Cong.* 11. Although none of Philo's lists of the encyclia is complete, the fact that astronomy is omitted so often has become a point of scholarly debate.[89] Critics have maintained either that astronomy lacks integrity as a science or that astronomy transcends mundane science. As I hope to make clear in the following sections, neither of these views is quite correct.

(i) *The view that astronomy lacks integrity as a science.* Perhaps the weaker of the two views of astronomy is the one which tends to minimize it. Colson tends toward this position in a note to *Cong.* 11:

> Astronomy of an elementary kind was regularly included among the En-cyclia, but is not named by Philo in his other lists of the subjects, doubt-less because, as often in other writers, it is regarded as a branch of geometry.[90]

In support of his view that astronomy should be considered as part of geometry, Colson cites Quintilian's treatment of the disciplines in *Institutio Oratoria*.[91] Philo and Quintilian, however, had different goals. Philo tends to view the world in terms of a comprehensive religious philosophy, while Quintilian is primarily concerned with the use of various disciplines to enhance the orator's skill. Quintilian is not committed to constructing a comprehensive picture of all the elements in the universe. These fundamental differences would seem to obviate the conclusions drawn by Colson.

One other observation might be adduced to support the notion that astronomy is subordinate to geometry: that is, the similarity between the two disciplines. This in itself is insufficient. For instance, Plato remarks that astronomy and music are "in some sort kindred sciences" (*Rep.* 530d); yet these disciplines still are distinct. Between various disciplines in the *quadrivium* there are real affinities, but this is a reflection of the nature of the sciences, rather than an argument for the primacy of the one at the expense of another.

Drummond also believes that Philo minimized astronomy. Or, to put it more precisely, Drummond first attributes that view to Philo; then, as the following passage indicates, Drummond takes him to task for his alleged position:

> It is especially curious to notice Philo's repeated attacks on astronomy. . . .
> We cannot but admit that they betray a certain narrowness of view, when
> we remember that he was living in the city where Eratosthenes . . . had
> decided that the earth was spherical . . . and where Hipparchus had con-
> structed his great catalogue of fixed stars. . . . These great pioneers of exact
> science were, in his view, only wasting their gifts upon barren speculations.
> For, in the first place, their inquiries contributed nothing to the true end of

human life. . . . In the second place, the questions with which astronomy deals are beyond the powers of human thought.[92]

Drummond's view is based on a superficial reading of certain passages in Philo, especially *Mig.* 184–89. Such passages are deceptively simple and potentially misleading.[93] Philo's actual position on astronomy is complex, for it depends, in large measure, on understanding an implicit distinction somewhat similar (yet not at all equivalent) to the modern distinction between astronomy and astrology. Drummond is partly correct; Philo does mount "repeated attacks." But what is attacked is the *perversion* of astronomical science as he knew it. There are limits in Philo's mind beyond which the astronomer goes only at the peril of becoming a worshipper of stars, a pantheist, a materialist, or an astral determinist—all of which are evil. To warn of dangers inherent in astronomy is not the same as to minimize the discipline. For while it is certainly true that professional astrologers waste their gifts on "barren speculations," this excess does not impugn the value of astronomy, properly studied.

One final comment on Drummond's views: astronomy is not unique in being beyond the powers of human thought. Each of the *quadrivia,* studied deeply enough, will appear limitless to mortal men. To be sure, Philo does say that astronomy teaches this lesson. He undoubtedly made a special point of mentioning astronomy because the heavens themselves appeared limitless and there was a special mystery surrounding the element from which the heavens were thought to have been composed. The other disciplines, however, took as their provinces other parts of God's cosmos and were likewise beyond human thought.

(ii) *The view that astronomy transcends mundane science.* If a closer reading of Philo does not support the view that astronomy lacks integrity as a science, neither does it substantiate the opposite tendency to elevate the discipline. According to Bréhier, for instance, astronomy should not be placed among the encyclical sciences: "It is rather the first step of wisdom."[94] There is, indeed, weighty evidence to uphold Bréhier's contention. We shall therefore first consider arguments which favor the belief that astronomy transcends the encyclia and then indicate the difficulties involved in maintaining that belief.

In a well-known passage (cited by Bréhier) Philo explains:

> For just as heaven, being the best and greatest (*kratiston*) of created things (*gegonotōn*), may be rightly called the king of the world of our senses, so the knowledge of heaven, which the star-gazers (*astronomountes*) and the Chaldaeans especially pursue, may be called the queen of the sciences (*basilida tōn epistēmōn, Cong.* 50).

This passage requires elucidation. What is in Philo's mind when he calls

heaven *kratiston* or "most excellent"? First of all, there are the revolutions of
the planets, the "unswerving ever-harmonious order which they never for-
sake" (*Spec.* ii.230). Secondly, Philo is aware of the effect of heavenly bodies on
the natural world: seasons, weather, floods, tides, and growing things on
earth—all of these fall within the astronomer's excellent science (*Opif.* 113).
Finally, Philo believes that the heavenly bodies have a special position in the
cosmos. In the beginning, they enabled men to compute the divisions of time
and learn the nature of number (*tēn arithmou physin, Spec.* i.91). (In the genea-
logy of the universe, then, astronomy is prior and therefore superior to
arithmetic.) The distinctive quality of the heavens is further emphasized in
Som. i.15-16 where Philo says that the cosmos is composed of four elements—earth, water, air, and heaven. The first three of these "are such as can
in one way or another be apprehended, but the fourth is universally held to be
beyond our powers of apprehension." Heaven, Philo says, "has sent to us no
sure indication of its nature" (*Som.* i.21).[95] Elsewhere we learn that the stars
themselves are "living creatures (*zōa*), but of a kind composed entirely of
Mind" (*Plant.* 12). This tendency to view the celestial bodies in a special light
culminates in Philo's ascription of divinity to the stars: "The stars are souls
divine (*theiai*) and without blemish throughout" (*Gig.* 8).[96]

Much debate has centered around Philo's passages which refer to the divinity of stars. Since even a qualified affirmation of their divinity would be an
argument in favor of the transcendent position of astronomy, we should consider this topic in detail. Wolfson takes these "divinity" passages as simple linguistic borrowings from Greek popular religion and argues that "in all of
them he [Philo] speaks in the name of somebody else, without committing
himself to the view he presents."[97] Wolfson's position on the divinity of stars is
vulnerable. As he realizes himself, *Gig.* 8 (cited in the previous paragraph) is a
damaging exception to his contention that Philo puts words about the divinity
of stars in the mouths of others.[98] Surely on such a momentous issue as the
ascription of divinity to stars, if Philo did have reservations, he would have
stated them openly.[99] Yet Philo, who elsewhere is so careful to draw lines
between true and false in astronomy, does not talk disapprovingly about the
divinity of stars.

Wolfson's reluctance to admit that the stars in Philo's heaven are actually
"divine" stems in part from his conviction that such an admission would pose
a threat to Philonic monotheism. Goodenough has suggested, however, that
Philo's belief in the divinity of the stars did not compromise his monotheistic
faith. Citing *Spec.* i.19, Goodenough argues:

> The point is not the existence of other beings, whom Philo is willing here
> and elsewhere to call "gods", but the fact that worship is due only to
> "absolute power". . . . The statement of Philo shows us Judaism in its most

essential position, not denying the existence of the lesser gods, but denying that they should be worshipped.[100]

Goodenough's interpretation preserves Philo's monotheism while at the same time it accounts for the literal ascription of divinity to the stars. On this reading, those who claim that astronomy transcends the mundane sciences have gained a powerful argument to support their contention. For if the stars in Philo are divine, even in a qualified sense, their study may reflect that divinity.[101]

Reading about heaven in Philo, we can almost see ecstasy possessing him and guiding his hand.[102] See, for example, *Jos.* 145:

> Everything there [heaven] remains the same and regulated by the standards of truth itself moves in harmonious order and with the grandest of symphonies; while earthly things are brimful of disorder and confusion and in the fullest sense of the words discordant and inharmonious, because in them deep darkness reigns while in heaven all moves in most radiant light, or rather heaven is light itself most pure and unalloyed. . . .

With such visionary comparisons between heaven and earth, it is no wonder that students of Philo began to elevate the position of astronomy. Yet despite such lyricism, despite the "divinity" of the stars, in the Philonic dichotomy between things of sense and things of spirit, heaven belongs to the senses. Nor is there any middle ground. In *Cong.* 50 (quoted earlier in this section) heaven was called "the best and greatest (*kratiston*) of created things (*gegonotōn*)."[103] Thus far, the adjective has been stressed. It is necessary to recall, however, that the substantive, *gegonotōn,* definitely links heaven to the world of becoming and the senses. Whatever else can be said about astronomy, it grows out of the empirical world and is no more than *primus inter pares.*[104] Philo himself was quite clear about the distinction between worldly astronomy and the higher reaches of being:

> Skill in the study of astronomy is acquired in one part of the world, (namely) in the heaven and in the revolutions and circlings of the stars, whereas wisdom (pertains) to the nature of all things, both sense-perceptible and intelligible (*QG* iii.43).

(iii) *Terminological considerations.* Concerning the words *astronomia* and *astrologia* Marrou has written: "In Latin, as in Greek, *astronomia* and *astrologia* were interchangeable terms and each of them designated in turn authentic 'astronomy' and superstitious 'astrology.'"[105] What Marrou really seems to be saying here is as follows: *astronomia* was used to signify what *we* now know is "truly scientific," but it could refer to what *we* regard as superstitious as well; the same is true of *astrologia*. Implicit in Marrou's formulation is a comparison between ancient astral speculations and the modern discipline of astronomy. But the investigation of this issue tends to obscure the fact that the ancients themselves made different distinctions between what *they* regarded as authentic and superstitious in astronomy.[106]

Although the term *astrologia* does not appear in the Philonic corpus and *astrologikos* is used but once (in *Abr.* 82),[107] the word *astronomia* appears frequently. According to the context, it may be used to denote either a legitimate encyclical study (as in *LA* i.57) or what Philo regards as a heresy.[108] The latter usage is worth illustrating:

> For the Chaldaeans were especially active in the elaboration of astrology (*astronomian*) and ascribed everything to the movements of the stars (*Abr.* 69).

In the passage quoted here, Colson's translation of *astronomia* with the pejorative word "astrology" captures Philo's intent. Elsewhere, however, Colson's translation of *astronomia* does not fit the context and seems either arbitrary or based on modern conceptions of what is authentic in astronomy and what is not.[109] The only explanation for Colson's inconsistencies is that he relied on intuition, not on an analysis of the content and limits of Philonic astronomy. We should therefore investigate in some detail Philo's actual beliefs concerning the relative values of various supraterrestrial speculations. Only with the contents and limits of Philonic astronomy before us, shall we be able to determine whether any particular appearance of *astronomia* refers to the encyclical discipline itself or to a practice of dubious legitimacy in Philo's eyes. As a possible aid to this study, we should discuss several other terms which could shed some light on the problem.

In speaking of Abram at one point, Philo uses the words *astrologikon kai meteōrologikon* (*Abr.* 82). Does the latter term regularly signify the inauthentic in Philo? An examination of the occurrences of *meteōrologia* and *meteōrologikos* reveals the same ambiguity which we found in the case of *astronomia*. On the one hand, Philo lists *meteōrologia* along with piety, holiness, ethics, kingcraft, etc., as positive accomplishments of the sage (*sophos, Ebr.* 92). Philo says that *meteōrologia* deals "with the air and the consequences which result through its changes and variations both at the main seasons of the year and those particular ones which follow cycles of months and days" (*Ebr.* 91)—a definition which we shall soon see is strikingly similar to that of authentic astronomy. On the other hand, we find *meteōrologia* used in connection with the most heretical excesses:

> The good bestowed in the past was his [Abraham's] departure from Chaldaean sky-lore (*meteōrologias*), which taught the creed that the world was not God's work, but itself God, and that to all existing things the vicissitudes of

better and worse are reckoned by the courses and ordered revolutions of the stars, and that on these depends the birth of good and ill (*Heres* 97).[110]

Meteōrologia and *meteōrologikos,* then, are not used systematically to designate what should be regarded as appropriate or inappropriate for the encyclical study.

We turn now to Philo's use of *chaldaikos* and related words.[111] In a passage from *De Congressu,* Philo clearly associates "the land of Chaldaea" with heavenly speculations which elsewhere are rejected with the whole force of his thought:

> For he [Nahor] does not remove from the land of Chaldaea, that is he does not sever himself from the study of astrology (*peri astronomian theōrias*); he honours the created before the creator, and the world before God, or rather he holds that the world is not the work of God but is itself God absolute in His power (*Cong.* 49).

Now Philo was aware that Chaldaeans were famous for their investigations into heavenly matters.[112] He was also aware of the heretical nature of Chaldaean theology which profanely likened the created to the Creator.[113] From these considerations, we might reasonably expect Philo's use of *chaldaikos,* etc., to denote astral speculations of which he disapproved. Again this expectation is not fulfilled.

If we examine other references to *chaldaikos* (and the like) and place them within the context of Philo's thought, it becomes clear that these terms do not always have a pejorative sense.[114] In *Heres* 289, Philo speaks of the "migration from the creed of the Chaldaeans to the creed of the lovers of God, that is, from the created and sensible to the intelligible and creative Cause." Naturally, the migration is depicted as a move to something good. We cannot infer, however, that this is a migration *from* wickedness, vice, or heresy. It is simply a move from the created to the intelligible world. Philo cannot denigrate the created world because it is God's own creation. Nor can he denigrate Chaldaea because Abraham once sojourned there. Although the patriarch had not, as yet, come to knowledge of God, his life in Chaldaea was virtuous and his sojourn there, a necessary part of his spiritual development.[115]

Other passages, placed within their respective contexts, also point to the conclusion that the terms *chaldaikos,* etc., do not distinguish the authentic from the inauthentic.[116] Since we have no reliable linguistic guide, we shall now try to make this distinction based on expository passages concerning lessons which may be learned from heavenly investigations. These passages, supplemented by other references to his thought, should reveal the extent of astronomy for Philo.

(iv) *Limits of Philonic astronomy.* As in the case of arithmetic and arithmology, we may construct a continuum of heavenly speculations. The "scientific" end of the continuum consists of a body of material which both Philo and moderns would consider "astronomical." Moving to a more ambiguous realm, we find material which Philo incorporates in the encyclical study of astronomy, but which a modern scientist would reject as fanciful or "astrological." Finally, there are beliefs which Philo dismisses with contempt. Although these beliefs are not labeled with unambiguous pejorative terms, they could never have been part of astronomy proper, as Philo conceives of it. My aim here is to draw the lines between these three categories.

To begin with the primary concern of the astronomer, Philo says that "skill in the study of astronomy is acquired in one part of the world, (namely) in the heaven and in the revolutions and circlings of the stars . . ." (*QG* iii.43). Elsewhere Philo indicates that other interests of the astronomer are to investigate

> the size of the sun and its courses, how it regulates the seasons of the year by its revolutions as it advances and retreats at the same rate of speed . . . also the different illuminations of the moon, its phases, its waning and waxing, and the movement of the other stars both in the fixed and the planetary order (*Mut.* 67).

Investigations of the sort outlined above sound familiar to modern ears. The student of astronomy does more: he perceives "timely signs of coming events." By the movement of heavenly bodies,

> men conjecture future issues, good harvests and bad, increase and decay of animal life, fair weather and foul, gales and calms, floodings and shrinkings of rivers, seas smooth and rough, irregularities of the seasons. . . . Indeed it has happened that, by conjecture based on the movements of the heavenly bodies, men have notified in advance a disturbance and shaking of the earth, and countless other unusual occurrences, proving the complete truth of the words, "the stars were made for signs" (*Opif.* 58–59).

The events mentioned here would appear to be divided between what modern commentators would call "astronomical" (e.g., the influence of the heavens on the tides) and "astrological."[117] But Philo did not think of any of these investigations as false (leading to heresy), unnecessary, or inappropriate to the discipline of astronomy. Signs, in particular, are important because "of all the things that happen upon earth, the signs are graven in the face of heaven" (*Spec.* i.92). The philosophical justification for the study of stars is not difficult to find, for like the Chaldaeans Philo believed in a "sympathetic affinity" between the parts of the cosmos (*Mig.* 178–79).[118] Since, on this view, the universe is a unity, the heavens can reasonably be thought to reflect events on earth.[119]

The most familiar astral signs of antiquity were the signs of the zodiac.

Philo mentions them more than once in connection with both the tribes of Israel[120] and the precious stones on the breastplate (*ephod*).[121] Whether or not these signs figured significantly in a Cosmic Mystery, as Goodenough argues,[122] it is certain that Philo thought they could not be ignored by students of the natural world: "For each of the signs of the zodiac also produces its own particular colouring in the air and earth and water and their phases, and also in the different kinds of animals and plants" (*Mos.* ii.126). Philo never hints that the zodiac is not part of astronomy as he understood it. Philo's only reservation grew out of his commitment to monotheism. The signs of the zodiac could never become actual objects of worship as they were for the historical Chaldaeans.[123] The zodiac might foretell certain events; it was not the author of them.[124]

If the stars do not cause events, they also do not rule the lives of men (*Mig.* 181). Good and ill are not determined by the revolutions of the heavens (*Heres* 97). These points are indicative of a concerted attack made by Philo on astral determinism. The attack is officially directed against the Chaldaeans, who in fact held that there was a necessity which ruled even the gods.[125] According to Wolfson, Philo's real targets were the Stoics for, while Philo agreed with the Stoics that "'causes have their sequence, connexion and interplay,' unlike them, he did not represent 'fate and necessity as the cause of events.'"[126] Philo's insistence that the will of man is free from the domination of the stars is based on ethical and theological considerations.[127] The least tincture of astral determinism would wreak havoc on Philo's philosophical system[128] and, therefore, must be considered beyond the limits of the discipline of astronomy.

The student of astronomy who does not understand the limits of his discipline may follow any one of several paths into heresy. We have already seen that Philo accepts the signs of heaven as a meaningful part of astronomy. To attribute to them too much power would not be difficult. The result, as Philo knew, was the error of believing in astral determinism. Materialism likewise arises in the poorly educated student. He might begin his studies by noting the majesty and harmony of heaven. Overwhelmed, he might conclude his studies, like the impious builders of the Tower of Babel, in the belief that "nothing exists beyond this world of our sight and senses" (*Som.* ii.283).

Philo believes that once one has studied the arts and sciences, particularly astronomy, one must arrive at a belief in the Creator. The atheist simply does not make the proper inference; he does not understand the argument for the existence of God from the design of the universe. In *QG* ii.34, Philo gives what would be a proper sequence of thoughts for the truly educated astronomer:

[Sight] first cut and made the road to philosophy. For when it sees the movements of the sun and moon, and the wanderings of the other planets, and the inerrant revolution of the entire heaven, and the order which is above all description, and the harmony, and the one true certain Creator of the world, it reports to its only sovereign, reason, what it has seen. And this (reason), seeing . . . through them the higher paradigmatic forms and the cause of all things, immediately apprehends . . . that visible nature did not come into being by itself. . . . But it is necessary that there be some Creator and Father. . . .

The last heresy which grows out of astronomy is pantheism. It occurs as a result of the false identification of created and Creator. Philo depicts the Chaldaeans adopting this position—most likely, a reference to the Stoics.[129] An example of pantheistic thought may be found in *Abr.* 69:

> While exploring numerical order as applied to the revolution of the sun, moon and other planets and fixed stars, and the changes of the yearly seasons and the interdependence of phenomena in heaven and on earth, they concluded that the world itself was God, thus profanely (*ouk euagōs*) likening the created to the Creator.[130]

Unlike other heretics mentioned earlier, pantheists were inclined to worship. They erred in that instead of praying *with* the universe, pantheists prayed *to* the universe.[131]

This concludes our analysis of the queen of the sciences. The study of astronomy is fraught with dangers, some of which we have indicated here. Yet the rewards are great: of all the encyclia one could least afford to be ignorant of astronomy, for it primes man for his communion with God.

An Epilogue. The seven disciplines we have just surveyed constitute the basic units of this study. Each discipline has a history in its own right. If we had traced the disciplines back to classical times, we would have found, *inter alia,* that Philo's conceptions of arithmetic and geometry were influenced by Neo-Pythagorean thought. We also would have discovered subtle internal relationships within the *trivium* and the *quadrivium.* For example, from at least the time of Pythagoras investigators of the physical world were aware of the close relationship between mathematics and music, for it was clearly seen that mathematical ratios lay behind certain musical intervals. But did Philo actually make a substantive contribution to any one of the disciplines? Philo's contribution was not on this level. To be sure, his use of arithmology in allegories and his concept of truth and error in astronomy might warrant some mention in comprehensive analyses of the disciplines themselves. Yet such issues are not so telling as the impact on Hellenistic Jewish culture which the arts and sciences made, taken together, as the *enkyklios paideia.*

Chapter 2

The Encyclia in Context

Thus far the encyclia have been considered as individual studies. The problems we encountered were inherent either in the disciplines themselves or in Philo's conception of them. In this chapter, our concern will be to place the encyclia as a whole within the larger context of Philo's thought.[1] The major areas to be discussed here are the historical, philosophical, and pedagogical dimensions of secular education.

1. Historical Considerations

The Encyclia in Practice. Students of ancient education have debated in a general way, and without reference to Philo, whether an encyclical syllabus was followed in antiquity. Festugière, for instance, has taken the view that such a course of study was in use.[2] Marrou has argued the opposite, maintaining that "such a syllabus was hardly more than an ideal, and was only rarely and imperfectly realized in practice."[3] Philo's own writings do not indicate in an unequivocal way whether his interest was practical or theoretical. Several passages have a bearing on the issue; the first is *Cong.* 74–76. Since this is one of the few times that Philo speaks in the first person, we should quote the passage at length:

When first I (*egō goun*) was incited by the goads of philosophy to desire her I consorted in early youth with one of her handmaids, Grammar, and all that I begat by her, writing, reading and study of the writings of the poets, I dedicated to her mistress.

And again I kept company with another, namely Geometry, and was charmed with her beauty, for she shewed symmetry and proportion in every part. Yet I took none of her children for my private use, but brought them as a gift to the lawful wife.

Again my ardour moved me to keep company with a third; rich in rhythm, harmony and melody was she, and her name was Music, and from her I begat diatonics, chromatics and enharmonics, conjunct and disjunct melodies, conforming with the consonance of the fourth, fifth or octave intervals. And again of none of these did I make a secret hoard, wishing to see the lawful wife a lady of wealth with a host of servants ministering to her.

At first glance, *Cong.* 74–76 appears to be an autobiographical fragment from which we might infer that Philo had some sort of encyclical training. Wolfson, nevertheless, denies its personal character, claiming that although Philo's discussion could be a reflection of the school where he was educated, more likely it was not drawn from actual experience. The explanation advanced by Wolfson is that the passage is "merely a restatement of the Stoic theories of the order of studies for the purpose of making use of them in his allegorical interpretation of the scriptural story of Sarah and Hagar."[4] While we may grant, with Wolfson, that Philo may be embellishing an allegory here, this possibility does not vitiate the autobiographical nature of the passage.[5] Indeed, indications in the passage itself suggest that the author is speaking autobiographically.[6] In the absence of compelling evidence to the contrary, then, we should accept Philo's first-person statements concerning his education as we would those of other classical authors.[7] For no scholar has suggested that *De Congressu* was written for apologetic motives, and it is difficult to imagine what could have induced Philo to misrepresent his secular education to the inner circle of coreligionists who were likely to read the treatise.[8] The passage probably is what it appears to be—a record of Philo's own experience with the encyclical studies.

Philo's treatise *De Specialibus Legibus* also contains a passage which, while not autobiographical, suggests that encyclical studies were an accepted part of Alexandrian education. In discussing the benefactions of parents, Philo states that children should be given "not only life, but a good life" (*Spec.* ii.229). This includes training of the body carried out in the gymnasium as well as training of the soul achieved "by means of letters and arithmetic and geometry and music and philosophy as a whole which lifts on high the mind lodged within the mortal body" (*ibid.*, 230).

The Philonic passages which imply that there was an encyclical curriculum for the Jews to follow are admittedly sparse. This fact in itself does not argue against the hypothesis that some Jews were involved in the study of secular disciplines, for Philo says even less about the religious education of his community.[9] Yet Philo's knowledge of Scripture, Jewish custom and law speaks eloquently for the existence of an effective system of religious learning, and his virtual silence concerning the actual systems of education may simply indicate that these were so familiar as to be taken for granted. Furthermore, Philo's references to secular education, when considered together, bear the traces of practical concerns. For instance, Philo warns potential students against the dangers which the encyclia might hold in store for the unwary. If no students actually aspired to encyclical knowledge, there would have been no reason to enter into such circumstantial detail.

Class Division. Although we may conjecture that the encyclia were actually studied, only a small proportion of the Jewish population could have submitted to their rigors. In prescribing the liberal arts and sciences, Philo had in mind only men of the Jewish upper classes.[10] We shall also see that lower-class Jews neither received nor were in a position to receive encyclical education.

Since Philo's affiliation to the Jewish upper class is well-documented, we need not rehearse all the particulars of his family's material good fortune.[11] Several passages from the Philonic corpus suffice to place their author in the aristocracy. It has been suggested, for instance, that Philo is alluding to his own riches when Sarah speaks of Abraham's wealth as being "not on the usual scale of immigrants, for in this we now outshine those of the native inhabitants who are noted for their prosperity" (*Abr.* 252).[12] Another indication of Philo's station in life may be seen in his reflection that the administration of one's domestic life requires slaves (*Spec.* ii.123).[13] But the passage which reveals Philo's awareness of class distinctions among Jews most clearly is found in his treatise *In Flaccum*. Here Philo laments that during the pogrom of 38 C.E. certain prerogatives of aristocratic Jews were abrogated. What incensed Philo was that "commoners among the Alexandrian Jews, if they appeared to have done things worthy of stripes, were beaten with whips . . . suggestive of freemen and citizens" while, at the same time, magistrates from the upper class and members of the Jewish council of elders (*gerousia*) "whose very name implies age and honour, in this respect fared worse than their inferiors and were treated like Egyptians of the meanest rank and guilty of the greatest iniquities" (*Flac.* 80).

This passage illustrates class distinctions among Jews which are also apparent from Tcherikover's collection of contemporary papyri. The sums of money mentioned in that group of legal and business documents from Jews in Alexandria (dated in the reign of Augustus) are "always small, whether given as dowries or bequeathed as legacies or loaned. . . . These small sums imply poor circumstances, and we may infer that these people whose life was dependent upon sums so small were earning a living by 'the sweat of their brow.'"[14] The Jewish wet-nurses and their coreligionist, a serving maid, whose existences are recorded in the papyri definitely were part of the "lower stratum of the Jewish population of Alexandria."[15] Obviously these people, comprising the majority of the Jewish population,[16] were in no economic position to provide their children with the benefits of gymnastic and encyclical training. Membership in the gymnasium "was an expensive luxury reserved for the rich."[17] Like the suitors of Penelope, the Jews of Alexandria who devoted themselves to ordinary studies clearly must have had the resources and leisure to do so.[18]

Lower-class Jews not only lacked the basic prerequisites for an encyclical education; they also seem to have been opposed to it in principle. Indeed, Tcherikover maintains that there was "something like an ideology of the rich and an ideology of the poor."[19] Surrounded by a different social setting and guided by different cultural ideals,[20] the Jews of the lower classes seem to have shunned the "good life" with all that that implied for Philo. Realistically enough, they appear to have lacked the ambition which motivated some upper-class Jews in their quest for a secular education: that is, accommodation to the Greek aristocracy with a view to acquiring civic rights in Alexandria.

Women comprised another sector of the Jewish population which would not have taken a formal part in the study of the arts and sciences. The picture which Philo transmits to us of Alexandrian Jewish women is one of seclusion and devotion to the domestic arts.[21] It is thus with a sense of outrage that Philo describes the violation of feminine modesty in the pogrom of 38 C.E. Jewish women, he says, who had "avoided the sight of men, even of their closest relations, were displayed to eyes, not merely unfamiliar, but terrorizing through the fear of military violence" (*Flac.* 89). In times of peace, the Alexandrian Jewish woman had little of the "freedom of movement" which has been attributed to her Biblical counterpart.[22] In one passage, Philo writes:

> Market-places and council-halls and law-courts and gatherings and meetings where a large number of people are assembled, and open-air life with full scope for discussion and action—all these are suitable to men both in war and peace. The women are best suited to the indoor life which never strays from the house. . . . A woman, then, should not be a busybody, meddling with matters outside her household concerns, but should seek a life of seclusion (*Spec.* iii.169–71).

If we may take these prescriptions as reflecting a general climate of opinion in aristocratic Jewish circles, then it is doubtful that women were able to avail themselves of encyclical education. The modesty expected of Jewish women would have made their participation in advanced studies impossible—either those sponsored by a public institution or those arranged at home with a pedagogue.

In addition to the restraints of modesty, Philo's conception of the nature of women virtually excludes them from higher education. With the exception of the matriarchs, women in Philo are thoroughly depreciated; frequently they symbolize aspects of the irrational soul, either sense-perception or particular evils and vices.[23] There are also a "considerable number of passages where Philo simply affirms the inferiority of the female to the male."[24] For the most part, womankind is considered spiritually adolescent and, in consequence, incapable of grasping the encyclia. Heinemann remarks that several authors in antiquity, having realized that a certain amount of education was the necessary basis for full humanity, "recommended the admission of women to spiritual training."[25] Philo clearly was not among these authors.[26]

Auspices. Having considered various cultural and social factors related to encyclical study, we should ask whether Jewish youths undertook their secular training in Greek or Jewish institutions. The consensus of contemporary scholarly opinion is that Alexandrian Jews had access to Greek education as offered in the gymnasium. According to Hengel, for instance, only on the basis of this assumption can we understand "the remarkable and probably historically unique fusion of Jewish and Hellenistic culture in Alexandria from the third century B.C."[27] Nevertheless, any treatment of the question of the auspices of secular studies has to come to terms with the view, argued most strenuously by Wolfson, that all education for Jews was in institutions under Jewish control. Since Wolfson offers a number of arguments to support this claim we should discuss his position in some detail.

Wolfson contends that the two primarily Greek institutions of higher learning, the gymnasia and ephebea, were religious by nature. From these institutions, Egyptians were excluded "and so undoubtedly were also Jews."[28] While there is no doubt that the gymnasia and ephebea were under the aegis of Greek religion, Wolfson's other contentions prompt several topics for discussion. First, there is the issue of the Egyptians' exclusion from these institutions. Secondly, there is the inference that since the Egyptians were excluded, the Jews must have been denied entry as well. Thirdly, a question arises: since these institutions were religious in nature, would Alexandrian Jews have scrupled to participate in the activities of the gymnasia?

Concerning the first of these issues—Wolfson's statement that native Egyptians were excluded from the gymnasia—it should be stressed that this applied primarily to the Roman period. During the reign of the Ptolemies, those Egyptians who could afford a Greek education seem to have been able to acquire one.[29] According to A. H. M. Jones, at the end of the Ptolemaic period, membership of the gymnasia probably was "socially uniform, consisting of the well-to-do Hellenized class, but racially very mixed, including besides such families as had preserved their Greek blood unmixed a large number of half-caste and Hellenized Egyptian families."[30] Non-Greek foreigners, including Persians and Jews, were even better able to enjoy the benefits of Greek education.[31]

With the advent of Roman rule, Egyptians seem to have been excluded from the gymnasia for political reasons. In brief, Augustus sought to distinguish between Greek and non-Greek inhabitants of the city. Those who were classified as Greeks were given certain privileges; they "were made partners in the institutions of local government and were regarded as civilized people."[32] Those considered non-Greek were made to bear the weight of taxation. To this end a poll-tax (*laographia*) was instituted. The Egyptians appear to have paid the poll-tax without protest and to have accepted the cultural derogation entailed by its imposition. Rather than be grouped together with the Egyptians, however, upper-class Alexandrian Jews began a vigorous campaign for civic rights.[33] At least one papyrus (*CPJ* No. 151) has survived in which a Jew petitions that the poll-tax imposed on him be rescinded. But even if the Jews did not contest the humiliating tax in significant numbers, they contravened the spirit of the Roman distinction between Greeks and non-Greeks by trying to enter the gymnasia and ephebea.

Not all Jews who entered the gymnasia were seeking Greek education for its own sake. At least some were using these institutions and the education they offered for acquiring greater social mobility. The Jewish petitioner in *CPJ* No. 151 stresses in his request to be free of the poll-tax that he had received "the appropriate education (*tēs areskousēs paideias*) as far as my father's means allowed."[34] Philo himself was aware of social "incentives" to learning, as he indicates in *LA* iii.167:

> The day is a symbol of light, and the light of the soul is training (*paideia*). Many, then, have acquired the lights in the soul for night and darkness, not for day and light; all elementary lessons (*propaideumata*) for example, and what is called school-learning (*ta enkyklia legomena*) and philosophy itself when pursued with no motive higher than parading their superiority, or from desire of an office under our rulers.[35]

This passage is of interest to us for the insight it gives into the motives of a segment of Alexandrian Jewry; it also provides a setting within which Jewish learning of the encyclia becomes plausible. For an institution to have been useful in obtaining an office under the secular authorities of Alexandria, it would almost certainly have had to be Greek. Indeed, if Jews had studied Greek culture in special Jewish schools, they would have undermined their own best efforts to gain the favor of their rulers and to accomplish their social objectives.

In spite of Philo's disapproval, it is unlikely that many Jews would have deliberately submitted themselves to the disciplines without, at the same time, having been able to reap the social benefits which their study could provide. As long as the possibility for emancipation remained, there was sufficient reason for Jews to enter Greek institutions for encyclical instruction. That Jews did in fact continue to ply this route during the first decades of the present era is obvious not only from Philo's writings, but also from the Edict of Claudius which was decreed in 41 C.E. This imperial edict seems to have been designed to resolve the question of the status of Jews in Alexandria. The most significant part for our purposes is Claudius' statement that the Jews must put an end to their practice of "intruding themselves" into institutions which were considered alien, "in a city not their own."[36] Behind this prohibition lies a practice; the edict itself suggests that Jews had been making their presence felt in Greek institutions of higher learning.

In view of the Jews' active struggle for emancipation, their situation must have differed in fact, if not in theory, from that of the Egyptians. Hence for Wolfson to draw parallels between the downtrodden Egyptians and Jews who were animated by the hope of emancipation is surely an error, for during the period in question these two ethnic groups appear to have been guided by different stars.

We may consider at this point how the religious nature of the gymnasium affected Jews of Philo's convictions. Feldman has described the atmosphere of the gymnasium:

> All the gymnasia had numerous busts of deities, particularly of Hermes and Heracles, the patron gods of the gymnasium. The gymnasium itself was dedicated to one or more of these deities, so that, for example, we hear of one that was dedicated to Ammon, Pan, Apollo, Hermes, and Heracles. These statues were not mere adornments in the gymnasium. . . . The games in which the students of the gymnasia participated were religious festivals. . . .[37]

Far from avoiding the gymnasium, however, Philo appears to have witnessed contests there, as *Provid.* 58, *Prob.* 26, and *Prob.* 141 indicate.[38] *Mig.* 116 also reveals a familiarity with the gymnasium. In this passage, Philo mentions various important educational influences on a man's life, such as the home tutor (*paidagōgos*), the school master (*didaskalos*), and parents. Included in the list is the *sōphronistēs*. Colson proposes that this term is an allusion to the "Athenian office of *sōphronistai*, officials appointed to look after the morals of the Ephebi in general and particularly in the gymnasia."[39] For our purposes, Marrou adds a critical point:

> In the fourth century the administration of the ephebia was . . . guaranteed by the introduction of a committee of "controllers of wisdom"—*sōphronistai*. . . . This committee disappeared at some unknown date in the Hellenistic period, but it began to function again under the Empire. . . .[40]

This remark raises the possibility that Philo is alluding to the *sōphronistēs* not as an Athenian functionary, but as a contemporaneous official of the local gymnasium. In either case, the conjunction of the *sōphronistēs* with other persons of obvious value in a system of education suggests that Philo was well-disposed toward the gymnasium.

As a further indication that Philo did not regard the gymnasium as an institution to be avoided, we should consider part of his interpretation of Deut. 25:11–12. In *Spec.* iii.176, Philo praises "the managers of gymnastic competitions" (*tous tōn gymnikōn agōnōn athlothetas*) for barring women from these spectacles. There is no hint here that Philo had any reservation in principle about the gymnasium or the competitions held there. In fact, he goes out of his way to praise the officials of the institution, for the rules they established coincided with his reading of Scripture.

On the surface, there seems to be something paradoxical about Philo's position with regard to the gymnasium. In Feldman's view,

> Because of the religious associations of [athletic] contests, even participation as a spectator involved a compromise with orthodoxy; and yet Philo himself, who is always so careful to maintain his orthodoxy, has almost an expert's knowledge of boxing and seems to have attended chariot races as well.[41]

The paradox becomes somewhat less acute when we think in terms of an Alexandrian Judaism based on a *modus vivendi* worked out during the long settlement of Jews in Egypt.[42] From all indications, Philo maintained a delicate balance between what was later embodied in "rabbinic tradition" and the exigencies of life in Alexandria. For example, in *Mos.* ii.211 Philo argues that the leisure of the Sabbath should not be spent "in bursts of laughter or sports or shows of mimes or dancers. . . ." Tacit approval seems to have been given to Jewish participation in these pagan activities on weekdays, but the line was drawn there. For while scope was given for Jews to take an active role—as they undoubtedly did—in the popular culture of Alexandria, the Jewish day of rest was to remain hallowed. Hengel has indicated how these issues, which raise the spectre of assimilation, may be resolved. As he says, the involvement of Diaspora Jews in things Greek need not be taken "without qualification as an evasion of Jewish belief; partly, it is also a sign that the Judaism of the Diaspora had won an inner self-assurance over against its polytheistic environment."[43]

The synagogues which flourished in this environment provided a center not only for communal prayer, but also for instruction. As Philo reports, "Each seventh day there stand wide open in every city thousands of schools of good sense, temperance, courage, justice and the other virtues . . ." (*Spec.* ii.62). In *Mos.* ii.216, Sabbath schools are again mentioned:

> The Jews every seventh day occupy themselves with the philosophy of their fathers, dedicating that time to the acquiring of knowledge and the study of the truths of nature. For what are our places of prayer throughout the cities but schools of prudence and courage and temperance and justice and also of piety, holiness and every virtue by which duties to God and men are discerned and rightly performed?

Examining the nature of this instruction, we find that *Spec.* ii.62 and *Mos.* ii.216 emphasize theological and ethical issues—"duties to God and men," respectively.[44] Likewise, in *Opif.* 128 Philo says that God bids men to devote their Sabbaths to philosophy "with a view to the improvement of character and submission to the scrutiny of conscience." The impression gained from these passages is that secular studies would not have fit in the curriculum of the Sabbath schools.

Spec. ii.63–64 strengthens this impression. In that passage, Philo distinguishes between the Sabbath and weekdays. On the seventh day, the soul is active, and the faithful concentrate on "theoretical" matters which fall under two main categories: "one of duty to God as shewn by piety and holiness, one of duty to men as shewn by humanity and justice" (*Spec.* ii.63). These pursuits are associated with "knowledge and perfection of the mind" (*ibid.*, 64).[45] The studies which are appropriate to weekdays, on the other hand, are characterized by the opposites of the aforementioned qualities. In accordance with the typology invoked by Philo here, these studies are "practical" as opposed to "theoretical"; akin to the body, not the spirit. The encyclia match this description, for Philo frequently remarks upon their practical qualities as well as their affinities to the material world. The encyclia also are clearly associated with conjecture and progress as distinct from knowledge and perfection.[46] To be sure, Philo never states explicitly that the encyclia were to be studied exclusively on weekdays. But *Spec.* ii.63–64 makes it clear that it would be inappropriate for them to be discussed on the Sabbath.

There are other indications that Sabbath studies were not encyclical in nature. For instance, we may infer from *Spec.* ii.62 that Sabbath schools attracted a large part of the Jewish community. Encyclical education, with its limited social function and appeal, could not command such an audience. *Hypoth.* 7:11–13 suggests that the observant masses of Jews did not want to be ignorant of Jewish law. Concentrating their efforts on "ancestral laws and customs," the masses in all probability did not direct their attention to the more esoteric encyclia. All the evidence then points to a Sabbath school curriculum which was ethical, theological, or exegetical in nature.[47] It is highly unlikely that the Jewish community provided both spiritual curriculum on the Sabbath and a secular one at other times. And since there is no evidence that synagogue schools were open on weekdays,[48] we may conclude that if the Jews encountered secular studies in an institutional setting, it would have been in the Greek gymnasium.

2. Metaphysical and Epistemological Framework

The purpose of this section is to place the encyclia within the larger framework of Philo's philosophical reflections. We have already observed that each of the arts detaches items from the world of nature (*Cong.* 144).[49] How then does Philo view that world which supplies the student of the encyclia with primary data? Unfortunately, there is no univocal answer to this question, for

Philo treats the material world in such a varied way that Baer was able to assemble Philonic opinions regarding it under two contrary headings. First, Baer presents Philo's positive orientation toward the created world:

> Although the categorical qualitative distinction between God and the created world is presupposed throughout his writings, nonetheless Philo not infrequently emphasizes that the world was made by God and therefore is good and beautiful. Such a positive evaluation of the created world is seen particularly in [De Opificio Mundi], where Philo's descriptions of the handiwork of nature and of the harmony, symmetry, and beauty of the created world are almost poetic in quality. . . .[50]

Following this, Baer outlines Philo's negative orientation toward the created world:

> . . . Far more typical of Philo's writings as a whole are those passages where the created world is portrayed as hostile and antithetic to the good life. No longer is a relationship of moderation towards sense-perception, pleasure, and the body appropriate, since these are realities evil in themselves and therefore to be shunned entirely.[51]

In discussing these seemingly irreconcilable positions, Baer suggests that the influence of the Old Testament is decisive: where Philo relies more heavily on Scripture his view of the created world is more likely to be positive.[52]

While Baer's suggestion is helpful in explaining our author's divergent views of creation, another aspect of Philo's thought should also be mentioned in this regard: that is, his tendency to write from what appear to be opposing points of view.[53] Either he writes from within an ideal world, in which case he assumes the point of view of the perfected philosopher, or he writes in a more practical vein from the point of view of an ordinary man.[54] What is insignificant to the ecstatic Philo who can write with his soul fixed on virtue is not insignificant to the practical Philo who knows that few souls fly directly to the upper reaches of heaven. Philo's contrary opinions on the created world not only correspond nicely to, but also ultimately depend upon these different perspectives. For the philosopher, the created world is necessarily evil—a realm which the sage, in his perfection, transcends. Ordinary men, on the other hand, see the created world as a good, for only through knowledge of that world can they come to know God. These two types of men and their respective paths to knowledge will be portrayed in later chapters. At present, it is sufficient to observe that serious study of the encyclia entails a positive orientation toward the material world.

We should now consider in greater detail how a student of the encyclia apprehends the world.[55] It is immediately clear that Philo posits a close relationship between the encyclical disciplines and the organs of sense. As he says in *Cong.* 20–21:

The votary of the school studies (*tais enkykliois theōriais*), the friend of wide learning, must necessarily be associated with the earthly and Egyptian body [= Hagar]; since he needs eyes to see and read, ears to listen and hear, and the other senses to unveil the several objects of sense. . . . It is sense which judges the sensible. . . .[56]

Even those who eventually transcend encyclical studies must rely on the sense-organs, for without them "we cannot live, since they are needed for our training while in the life of the body" (*Heres* 315).[57]

Within the larger context of Philo's philosophy, the encyclia assume an intermediate position between mere opinion and pure knowledge.[58] Wolfson has formulated the degrees of Philonic knowledge in the following way:

We thus have in Philo a general twofold division of knowledge subdivided into three. (A) Knowledge of the senses, consisting of (1) sensation and opinion. (B) Knowledge of the mind, consisting of (2) rational knowledge, such as a knowledge of the various sciences which ultimately rests on sensation, and of (3) the knowledge of the ideas which does not rest on sensation at all.[59]

If we were to fill this scheme in, we could place nonencyclical *technai*, like the art of the charioteer, on the lowest level (A1). The encyclia clearly belong on the intermediate level (B2). The highest level (B3) is reserved for the insights of philosophy and wisdom itself.

While it is beyond the scope of the present work to indicate with precision the content of Philonic philosophy and wisdom, two passages shed some light on the relations between (B2) and (B3), as defined above. In *Opif.* 54–55, Philo describes a man who, having contemplated the heavenly panoply, then turns from astronomical (encyclical) concerns to philosophical ones:[60]

Banqueting on sights displayed to it one after another, his soul was insatiate in beholding. And then, as usually happens, it went on to busy itself with questionings, asking What is the essence of these visible objects? Are they in nature unoriginate, or had they a beginning of existence? What is the method of their movement? And what are the principles by which each is governed? It was out of the investigation of these problems that philosophy grew, than which no more perfect good has come into the life of mankind.[61]

The second passage, *Cong.* 79–80, contains Philo's formulation of the relationship of the encyclia to higher knowledge:

And indeed just as the school subjects (*ta enkyklia*) contribute to the acquirement of philosophy, so does philosophy to the getting of wisdom. For philosophy is the practice or study of wisdom, and wisdom is the knowledge of things divine and human and their causes.[62] And therefore just as the culture of the schools (*hē enkyklios mousikē*) is the bond-servant of philosophy, so must philosophy be the servant of wisdom.

This passage lends itself easily to the construction of a ratio and a hierarchy of knowledge: the encyclia are to philosophy as philosophy is to wisdom. Out of these considerations, a picture of intellectual development emerges. The process of abstraction begins when students of the encyclia appropriate parts of the sense-world (as in *Cong.* 144). As one's studies continue, the disciplines become more structured. Finally, questions of definition arise. At precisely that point, the encyclical disciplines reach their limits on the ascending epistemological scale, and philosophy enters.[63]

What cognitive claims may be made for this encyclical knowledge, which rests on sensation? An orthodox Platonist clearly would not assign the arts and sciences to the uppermost segment of the Divided Line.[64] Philo follows suit, often dissociating the encyclia from the concept of pure knowledge:

> "And so," says Abraham, "in the same degree as the mind is more powerful, more active and altogether better than the hand, I hold knowledge (*epistēmēn*) and wisdom (*phronēsin*) to be more admirable than the culture of the schools (*tēs enkykliou mousikēs*) . . ." (*Cong.* 156).[65]

Technically, within Philo's epistemological framework, the only insights which warrant the label "truths" are the verities of philosophy and wisdom.[66] The encyclia, relying as they do on the fallible senses, cannot lay claim to possessing the truth. As Philo explains in *Cong.* 142:

> We give the name of arts (*technas*) . . . to music, grammar, and the kindred arts, and accordingly those who by means of them reach fulness of accomplishment are called artists (*technitai*), whether they are musicians or grammarians; but we give the name of knowledge to philosophy and the other virtues, and that of men of knowledge to those who possess these virtues. Those only are prudent and temperate and philosophers who without exception do not err in the dogmatic conclusions belonging to that form of knowledge which they have mastered by their diligence in the way that the above-mentioned [artists] err in the more theoretical conclusions[67] of the lower arts (*mesōn technōn*).

While philosophical activities ideally produce truth, encyclical studies, which are dependent on sense perception, produce only conjecture and probability.[68] Philo is careful to make these distinctions. For instance, having reviewed various hypotheses concerning the nature of the heavens, Philo says that all the views "pertaining to heaven, that fourth and best cosmic substance, are obscure and beyond our apprehension, based on guess-work and conjecture (*stochasmois kai eikasiais*), not on the solid reasoning of truth" (*Som.* i.23).[69] In this astronomy is not alone, for in *Cong.* 140 he states more generally that the products of the encyclical disciplines can only be seen "dimly."[70]

Encyclical disciplines, then, are composed of probable or conjectural observations made by the senses. Each study should be conceived of as having a specific structure. This is evident from the Stoic definition of *technē* to which Philo subscribed: i.e., "a system of conceptions (*systēma ek katalēpseōn*)[71] coordinated to work for some useful end" (*Cong.* 141). Likewise, in *LA* iii.92 and *QG* iii.35, Philo mentions that the disciplines have principles (of organization); presumably these guarantee the coherence of the encyclia.

Before concluding this discussion of the philosophical context of the encyclia, I should like to point to one more feature of the disciplines—their ultimate unknowability. The most obvious explanation for the inability of men to learn the encyclia completely is summed up by the adage *brachus men gar ho bios, hē de technē makra.*[72] Philo expounds on this saying in *Som.* i.8–11.

> The ends pursued in the different branches of knowledge prove to be not only hard to reach, but absolutely beyond finding. That is why one man is a better scholar or geometrician than another, because no limit can be set to the extensions and enlargements of his subject in all directions. For what still remains is always waiting to engage us in fuller force than what we have already learned; so that the man who is supposed to have reached the very end of knowledge, is considered in the judgement of another to have come half way; while if Truth give her verdict, he is pronounced to be just beginning. For "life is short," said one, "and art is long";[73] and he best apprehends its greatness who honestly sounds its depths, and digs it like a well.

From this passage, we might infer that for Philo the major obstacle which stands between a man and full encyclical knowledge is the brevity of human life. This inference is mistaken, however, because the disciplines, as they are generally portrayed in Philo, are not simply long; they are infinite.

In order to understand the infinity of encyclical studies, we should note that Philo evokes the Platonic distinction between an ideal archetype and the multitude of things which participate in that ideal. Two passages are especially relevant:

> There are ever so many musical, grammatical and geometrical things, and just and prudent and courageous and temperate things, but music and grammar and geometry in the abstract . . . are each of them one thing, the original, the same as the archetypal idea (*mēden ideas archetypou diapheron*), and from this origin the many and indeed infinite particulars (*ta polla kai amythēta ekeina*)[74] have been formed (*Mut.* 146).
>
> When a musician or a scholar has died, the music or scholarship, that has its abode in individual masters, has indeed perished with him, but the original patterns (*ideai*) of these remain, and may be said to live as long as the world lasts . . . (*Det.* 75).

From these passages, it is clear that there are *ideai* of the encyclical disciplines. Perfect *ideai* cannot be reached by or reproduced in any particular student; the individual aspirant must be content with imperfect images. According to Philo, it is "enough for man" to possess "images (*eikonas*) . . . in the scale of number and magnitude far below the archetypes" (*archetypōn, Mut.* 183).

The archetypes to which Philo alludes are infinite in magnitude. Philo's conception of the infinity of the archetype is in harmony with and, indeed, may have been derived from the fact that for Philo all knowledge is God's.[75] Because of this, Philo says that only God can master a discipline: "Men are only said to have knowledge because they seem to know; whereas God is so called because He *is* the possessor of knowledge . . ." (*Mig.* 40). Indeed, it is "great ignorance to think that the soul of man can contain the unwavering, absolutely steadfast excellences of God" (*Mut.* 183). It is in this spirit, then, that Philo says in *Post.* 151–52:

> The wealth of the wisdom of God is unbounded and puts forth new shoots after the old ones, so as never to leave off renewing its youth and reaching its prime. For this reason all who imagine that they have arrived at the limit (*peras*) of any science (*epistēmēs*) whatever are perfect simpletons.

Similarly, Philo says that it is impossible to attain perfection in any *technē* (*Plant.* 81) and that the limit of science is "actually outside the range of human possibilities" (*Heres* 121). All these passages are significant to the student of the encyclia, for they indicate that he can, at best, look forward to concluding his pursuit with a limited amount of knowledge and with an appreciation for the infinity of God's disciplines.

3. Pedagogical Scheme

The Roles of God and the Student. What a philosophical analysis of the encyclia does not reveal is the extent of God's active involvement in the educational process. Readers of *De Opificio* are undoubtedly aware that the continued existence of the material world is dependent upon God's providence and his enduring good will.[76] Man's study of that world is also dependent on God's providence, for Philo writes: "Fallen is sense . . . unable of itself to perceive, were it not by a dispensation of God's saving providence set on its feet to the perception of material substances" (*Mut.* 56).[77] Despite the fact that sense perception is an imperfect mode of apprehension, God makes it possible simply because he is good,[78] and he loves to give.[79] Without diminishing his own perfection, God gives men the opportunity to learn the encyclia through the agency of the senses.

Underlying Philo's pedagogical reflections is a fundamental belief, expressed in *Som.* i.106–7, that there is an "irresistible impulse" (*akataschetō rhymē*) of man's "rational nature" (*logikēn physin*) toward education. Between God and man there is a dynamic interplay. No achievement is possible without God's gracious consent. For, "it is within the power of the teacher to lead us from one stage of progress to another; God only, Nature at its best, can produce in us the full completion" (*Fug.* 172). The deity then actively draws the mind of man up to Himself (*LA* i.38), and knowledge often "rids herself of grudging pride, runs out to meet the gifted disciples, and draws them into her company" (*Cong.* 122).

Several passages in Philo point to the fact that one's spiritual progress depends on the richness of his natural endowment. Two such passages may be given here:

> What is the beginning (*archē*) of the act of learning? Evidently it is the nature residing in the pupil with its receptivity towards the several subjects of study (*Fug.* 172).
>
> All that is heard or learned is a superstructure built on the foundation of a nature receptive of instruction, for if nature be not there to begin with all else is useless (*Mut.* 211).

As we shall see in our discussion of the patriarchs and Moses, God endows some rare individuals with full powers of intellect and spirit. More ordinary mortals are granted divine gifts, but in varying degrees. Differences in natural endowment are not a function of God's playing favorites. The fact that some men are more gifted than others—and all men are inferior in this regard to Isaac and Moses—is not owing to divine niggardliness, but rather to the capacity of particular men to receive: "For Him it is easy to bestow gifts, ever so many, ever so great, but for us it is no light matter to receive the proffered boons" (*Mut.* 218).[80] Whether the endowment be ample or sparse, God is the source of encyclical knowledge in the sense that he makes it possible for men to know. It is interesting, however, that man's imperfect nature itself is responsible for the ultimate imperfection of the knowledge which can be attained by him. This is clearly stated in *Aet.* 2:

> Now, if schooled in the doctrines of wisdom and temperance and every virtue we had scoured away the stains of the passions and soul-distempers, perhaps God would not have refused to impart the knowledge of things heavenly . . . to souls thoroughly purged and bright and radiant. But since we bear upon us deep ingrained the imprints of injustice and folly and other vices we must be content if through a study of probabilities[81] and by our own efforts we may discover some semblance of the truth.

Just as God bestows what is within the capacity of the recipient, so on a practical level Philo maintains that "teaching should be more abundant for the intelligent man, and less for the foolish man" (*QG* iv.102). In *Post.*

140–41, Philo speaks of the proper attitude a teacher should adopt on the issue of a student's capacity for learning:

> The teacher comes down to the learner and attentively studies him as one with whom he is intimately concerned. For teachers who when they set about giving their lessons keep in view their own great superiority[82] and not the capacity of their pupils, are simpletons, who are not aware how vast is the difference between a lesson and a display. . . . The man . . . who is setting out to teach, is like a good doctor, who with his eyes fixed not on the vastness of his science but on the strength of his patient, applies not all that he has ready for use from the resources of his knowledge—for this is end-less—but what the sick man needs, seeking to avoid both defect and excess.

This passage evokes a picture of the teacher choosing a course of moderation between the infinity of a discipline on the one hand, and the ability of a student on the other. Philo's concern for the plight of the student is, of course, evident here. That concern sometimes rises to the level of compassion, especially for diffident students.[83]

Ages of Man. In a chapter devoted to pedagogical considerations, it would be appropriate to determine the age at which a student should devote himself to the encyclia. The most comprehensive account of the stages of human development is found in *Opif.* 103–104, and is attributed to Solon the Athenian. Ten periods are enumerated, each seven years in length.[84] The first five periods in this scheme are characterized solely by physical manifestations. In the sixth period (beginning at age 35), "the understanding reaches its bloom." This is followed by the seventh period in which there is "progressive improvement and development of mind and reason" and the eighth (extending to age 56), in which mind and reason are perfected. While Philo does not use this opportunity to indicate when the encyclia might be most profitably studied, one feature of the account will appear elsewhere in Philo: i.e., the relatively advanced age at which full intellectual and spiritual development is reached.[85]

For a more detailed presentation of the years critical to education, we must turn to *Heres* 294–99 and *Cong.* 81–88.[86] Conflating these accounts, we find that the ages of man fall into four periods: childhood, adolescence, a borderline period (which will be our primary concern), and maturity.[87] The state of one's soul in the seven years of childhood "closely resembles smooth wax and has not yet received any impression of good or evil" (*Heres* 294). Unable to distinguish good from its opposite, the child "is reared with none but passions to be its comrades, griefs, pains, excitements, desires, pleasures, all of which come to it through the senses" (*Cong.* 81).[88]

During the second stage of life, one begins to apprehend both virtue and vice. At the outset, at least, the adolescent "chooses the worst" (*Cong.* 84).

Some learning takes place at this time; Philo calls it "the beginning of instruction" (*QG* iv.108) by which he may have meant such basics as the more elementary part of grammar. But it is clear that, without a more highly developed rational faculty, instruction cannot proceed very far. For the most part, in fact, Philo sees instruction during this period as potentially deleterious:

> The instructors to sin are legion, nurses and "pedagogues"[89] and parents and the laws of cities . . . which extol what should be derided; and apart from and before such instruction, the soul is its own pupil in the school of guilt, so that it is throughout weighed down by its capacity for producing ills (*Heres* 295).

The second stage is characterized by the emergence of a rudimentary rational faculty. It is a critical period because one enters it barely able to distinguish the good. And one should leave it, having put all temptation aside,[90] ready to submit to the rigors of encyclical education. Philo describes the transitions which one undergoes in this stage as follows:

> All we men, before the reason in us is fully grown, lie in the borderline between vice and virtue with no bias to either side. But when the mind is fully fledged when it has seen and absorbed into every part of its vitality the vision of the good, it ranges freely and wings its way to reach that vision and leaves behind . . . evil (*Praem.* 62).

In determining the age of a student who is passing from the second into the third period of his life, we need to refer to Gen. 16.3, which Philo read in the Septuagint: "So Sarah the wife of Abraham, ten years after Abraham dwelt in Canaan, took Hagar the Egyptian her handmaid and gave her to Abraham her husband as his wife." The period of ten years during which Abraham lived in Canaan is the second stage; the third stage, congress with Hagar, is the period of encyclical training. It is important to bear in mind that the Genesis text fixes the length of the second stage at ten years. We need not insist that the pre-encyclical (adolescent) stage had to last that long.[91] At the same time, Philo stresses that a student must be adequately prepared for his encounter with the encyclia:

> So then ten years after our migration to the Canaanites we shall wed Hagar, since as soon as we have become reasoning beings we take to ourselves the ignorance and indiscipline (*amathias kai apaideusias*) whose nature is so mischievous and only after a time and under (*en*[92]) the perfect number ten do we reach the desire for the lawful discipline which can profit us (*Cong.* 88).

The same theme appears in *Cong.* 121 where Philo says that "we cannot desire the training of the schools [the encyclia] the moment we become reasoning beings, as the understanding is still soft and flaccid." It is necessary, Philo continues, to harden our intelligence before mating with Hagar.[93]

Instruction proper—that is, instruction in the arts and sciences—begins at the age of 17, or thereabouts.[94] As Colson points out, according to Philo "the plan of forcing the Encyclia upon young boys really misses its aim."[95] How long is one to study the liberal arts and sciences before coming to spiritual maturity[96] in the fourth stage of life? No clear answer to this question is indicated because the length of the stage would vary from one student to the next. And, indeed, there was no guarantee that one would ever attain spiritual maturity.[97] But even in the best of circumstances men should not expect to become "heirs of wisdom"[98] in seven or ten years. Isaac does not marry until he is forty. Since marriage with Rebecca is taken by Philo to mean union with wisdom (*sophia*),[99] we should note that the final stage of life can follow more than twenty years of encyclical study:

> The fortieth year is the right time for the marriage of the wise man, for it is good (for him) to be trained and directed and abound in the right forms of discipline[100] in youth and to have regard for nothing else . . . (*QG* iv.154).

Twenty years of encyclia may in fact be a relatively short period. For passions continue to exist during the third stage; and, despite the fact that some men are able to control them, the acquisition of virtue is dependent upon having "lulled to rest the worst enemy of the soul" (*Sac.* 16). As the following passage indicates, victory over the passions, a *sine qua non* for the fourth age of man, is often a long-awaited event:

> When the prime is past, and the throbbing fever of the passions is abated, as though the storm winds had dropped, there begins in the man a late and hard-won calm (*Sac.* 16).

Encyclical Dangers. In discussing the individual encyclical disciplines, we noted certain perils which might catch the student unawares: Philo suggested that devotees of grammar and music might be seduced by the sound of words and melodies; rhetoric might be distorted into sophistry; and the risks run by the astronomer were considerable. But there are other stumbling blocks which students of the encyclia may encounter. These dangers are not associated with any specific discipline. Judging by the frequency with which he returns to the theme of failures in education, Philo was concerned lest the improper study of the disciplines should have an effect worse than ignorance of them.[101]

Perhaps Philo's main fear was that the student would become overly enamoured of the encyclia. To form a close bond with the object of one's study is quite natural.[102] To be so enthralled with the "splendour of the school studies" and the "attractive and seductive" (*QG* iii.23) qualities of the disciplines that one no longer found time to "unite" with wisdom is a danger.[103]

That danger is clearly expressed in *Cong.* 77–78—a passage in which the encyclia are depicted as the handmaids of philosophy:

> Some have been ensnared by the love lures (*tois philtrois*) of the handmaids and spurned the mistress, and have grown old, some doting on poetry, some on geometrical figures, some on the blending of musical "colours,"[104] and a host of other things, and have never been able to soar to the winning of the lawful wife. For each art (*technē*) has its charms, its powers of attraction, and some beguiled by these stay with them and forget their pledges to Philosophy.[105]

Exclusive acquaintance with the encyclia not only keeps a student away from higher pursuits; it also inclines him toward the heresy of believing that mind (*nous*), rather than God, has "leadership and sovereignty of human affairs" (*Spec.* i.334). In their pride, these heretics claim:

> It is mind which discovered the mechanical and the finer arts . . . which devised, fostered and brought to their consummation letters and numbers and music and the whole range of school studies (*tēn enkyklion hapasan paideian, Spec.* i.335–36).

Those who put ultimate trust in the powers of the mind come to grief, for they do not understand that *nous,* in conjunction with the senses, is only an *agent* for apprehending the encyclia. They fail to realize that God is the ultimate guarantor of the truth of encyclical thought.[106]

In *De Ebrietate,* Philo indicates two other dangers which are likely to beset the student of the encyclia. The issues addressed are when and when not to take up encyclical studies. Young men, Philo insists, must study the encyclia prior to philosophy. Allegorizing Rachel and Leah as the encyclia and philosophy, respectively, Philo stresses the nobility of Jacob's wish to unite initially with Rachel. This becomes the basis of a guideline for those aspiring to wisdom:

> The laws of human character as well as of nature agree with him [Jacob] in this; for Men of Practice must first take up with the younger culture [*neōtera paideia* = Rachel], that afterwards they may be able to have secure enjoyment of that which is more perfect. And therefore to this day the lovers of true nobility do not attend at the door of the elder sister, philosophy [Leah], till they have taken knowledge of the younger sisters, grammar and geometry and the whole range of the school culture (*tē sympasē tōn enkykliōn mousikē*). For these ever secure the favours of wisdom to those who woo her in guilelessness and sincerity (*Ebr.* 48–49).[107]

We should not suppose that this pedagogical advice is simply a reflection of Philo's need to allegorize the story of Rachel and Leah. Indeed, the conclusions are in accord with Philo's general principle that the "practical comes before the contemplative life. . . . For it is sheer folly to suppose that you will reach the greater while you are incapable of mastering the lesser" (*Fug.* 36–38).[108]

When should one not take up the encyclia? Philo's answer to this question bears the mark of a pedagogue who dealt with practical matters. In certain exceptional cases, men start the study of philosophy "from the very cradle . . . and afterwards deeming it wrong that they should have no tincture at all of the school subjects (*enkyklión*), bethink themselves to make a belated and painful effort to grasp them" (*Ebr.* 51). Philo's advice to these men is not to descend to the encyclical studies, for therein lies a danger of growing old in the company of inferior studies, losing "all power of retracing their course to the place from which they started" (*ibid.*). Thus what is essential in the education of the young becomes vanity in old age.[109]

Failures in Education. Philo delineates two kinds of ignorance in *Ebr.* 162–63:

> Now ignorance as a whole is of two different kinds; one single, that is complete insensibility, the other twofold, that is when a man is not merely the victim of a want of knowledge, but also, encouraged by a false idea of his own wisdom, thinks he knows what he does not know at all. The former is the lesser evil, for it is the cause of less serious and perhaps involuntary errors, and the second is the greater, for it is the parent of great iniquities, not only those which are involuntary, but such as are actually premeditated.

The first type of ignorance may be called "simple ignorance."[110] It is found in men who have "studied the lower subjects, but have been unable through dullness of nature to imbibe any knowledge" (*Sac.* 116). Lacking the requisite endowment, these men cannot grasp the principles of the encyclia. Their ignorance is considered involuntary and does not entail culpability. The second kind of ignorance involves moral responsibility. We find it in "the case of a man who is sufficiently intelligent to discern the truth, but, through self-regard, allows himself to be misled into a sophistical falsehood. . . ."[111] Since a student of this type is endowed with native ability, he is reprehensible if his studies should go awry.

LA iii.167–68 is explicit about some of the ways in which miseducation of responsible students might occur. According to that passage, they might acquire encyclical education "with no motive higher than parading their superiority, or from desire of an office under our rulers."[112] Philo makes it clear that he attaches blame to such actions, for he continues:

> The man of worthy aims sets himself to acquire day for the sake of day, light for the sake of light, the beautiful for the sake of the beautiful alone,

not for the sake of something else. . . . for this is the divine law, to value excellence for its own sake. The right principle, therefore, tests all aspirants as one does a coin, to see whether they have been debased in that they refer the soul's good to something external, or whether, as tried and approved men, they distinguish and guard this treasure as belonging to thought and mind alone (*LA* iii.167–68).

Borgen, perhaps the only contemporary scholar to consider the problem of miseducation in Philo, sees this passage in terms of the conflict between the sophists and the philosophers. From the time of Isocrates and Plato, Borgen says, the main issue between these schools was whether education "should serve practical aims in man's life."[113] The sophists maintained that education should so serve man. The philosophers, however, insisted that a "political and social career is not the objective of education. The objective is rather 'virtue' which is to be cherished for its own sake."[114] Borgen represents Philo as siding with the philosophers and thereby rejecting "such external things as luxurious living and political office as the proper goal of education."[115]

From Borgen's analysis, we might conclude that Philo consistently followed Stoic distinctions between the external and the internal and that the encyclia should only serve internal purposes which, in Philo's terms, means "belonging to thought and mind alone" (*LA* iii.168). According to this interpretation, miseducation occurs whenever the encyclia are placed in the service of anything other than virtue (or wisdom).

It is true that Philo condemned luxurious living and certain kinds of political ambition. We should not infer, however, that Philo's condemnation extended to all forms of political activity. Both Philo's words and his deeds suggest an attempt to strike a balance between the active and the contemplative life. As *Spec.* iii.1–6 indicates, Philo preferred to spend his time in contemplation. But occasionally he felt compelled to submit to "the ocean of civil cares." The embassy to Gaius is an example of Philo's active participation in politics.[116] Moreover, his writings provide numerous illustrations of the positive use of encyclical studies in the service of external goods. For instance, *Sac.* 78 implies that the disciplines in general and grammar in particular[117] promote a life of civic virtue.[118] Philo also associates the encyclia in general with such external goods as the conventions of law and custom. This association appears in the following allegory:

> I suggest, then, that the father is reason, masculine, perfect, right reason, and the mother the lower learning of the schools, with its regular course or round of instruction (*tēn mesēn kai enkyklion choreian te kai paideian*[119]). . . . Now right reason (*orthou logou*), the father, bids us follow in the steps of nature and pursue truth in her naked and undisguised form. Education (*paideias*), the mother, bids us give ear to rules laid down by human ordin-

ance, rules which have been made in different cities and countries and nations by those who first embraced the apparent (*dokēsin*) in preference to the true (*Ebr.* 33–34).[120]

Using the same allegorical equivalents already noted in *Ebr.* 33–34, Philo writes:

> Yet if our battalion be unable to do service to the father's commands and thus suffer defeat,[121] it will none the less have an ally in the mother, the lower education, who enacts from city to city the ordinances which custom and opinion approve . . . (Ebr. 64).

It is evident from these passages that Philo thought that the encyclia were crucial in the external task of educating men toward civic responsibility.[122] What is more, the encyclia also had another external value: a student could practice almost any of them as a vocation.[123] With the possible exception of rhetoric, the practitioners of which were largely sophists, the disciplines lead to respectable means of earning a livelihood.

Thus in delineating the uses and misuses of education, Philo did not assert that the encyclia should serve only the life of Stoic virtue. Neither political activities nor practical applications of the arts and sciences were condemned as inherently evil, although both were fraught with danger. But Philo drew the line when secular education compromised either the integrity of the individual or the solidarity of the Jewish community. It is not coincidental that in *LA* iii.167–68 the most explicit instances of miseducation are students who use the encyclia to serve pretentious ends or to curry favor with the Roman rulers.

Chapter 3

Philo's Typology of Mankind

In a passage which provides much food for thought, Philo writes that God "knoweth well the different pieces of his own handiwork, even before He has thoroughly chiselled and consummated them, and the faculties which they are to display at a later time, in a word their deeds and experiences" (*LA* iii.88). Two related issues arise from this passage. The first involves the general question of free will; from *LA* iii.88, at least, there would seem to be an aspect of determinism in Philo's philosophy.[1] The second has to do with Philo's conception that God has fashioned "different pieces," from which it is reasonable to infer that there are different types of men inhabiting Philo's world. Let us consider the latter issue first by asking what classifications of mankind emerge from Philo's works as a whole. In the hierarchy of knowledge according to Philo, what options are open to the members of the various classes of men? Having addressed ourselves to these questions, we shall see that the natural endowments of men influence the kind of education open to them.

1. Classifications

Philo was by no means the first ancient thinker to classify men. Without returning to Plato's classifications in the *Republic,*[2] we should consider Stoic conceptions of man. The primary Stoic distinction to bear in mind is that between the sage (*sophos*) and the ordinary man. As Long points out: "A rehearsal of the sage's characteristics will reveal that he never assents to what is false, never opines, never forgets and is ignorant of nothing (meaning 'never makes weak or changeable assents' [SVF III 548])."[3] On the basis of these observations, we might conclude that "the sage is in some way the criterion of truth or reality."[4] Further, the Stoic sage's emotional life is not marred by extreme affections such as desire, fear, pleasure and distress.[5] His life is rather characterized by "proper emotional states" (*eupatheiai*).[6] In his ethical life, the sage does everything "from full moral intentions and his conduct will be entirely consistent."[7]

This briefly is a sketch of the ideal man. The Stoics realized, however, that one does not generally achieve emotional and ethical perfection without a struggle. For that reason, they made room for another type of man, the *prokopton,* one in progress toward the goals of the sage. *Prokoptontes* are ordinary men who strive with more or less determination toward virtue.[8] Since the approach to human perfection is uncertain, it is necessary to have a classification like this, as a passage from Seneca indicates:

That which you mention is the mark of an already perfect man. . . . But the
approach to these qualities is slow, and in the meantime, in practical matters, the path should be pointed out for the benefit of one who is still short
of perfection, but is making progress. Wisdom by her own agency may perhaps show herself this path without the help of admonition; for she has
brought the soul to a stage where it can be impelled only in the right direc-
tion. Weaker characters, however, need someone to precede them, to say:
"Avoid this," or "Do that" (*Epistles* 94.50–51).[9]

The passage just cited not only sets forth the necessity for the category of
"progressive" men. It also alludes to a difference between the sage and the
ordinary man in their respective attitudes toward rules (*praecepta*). On this
theme Long reflects, "the wise man does not need *praecepta*, since he does not
act by external rules, but by his internal *logos*, therefore it is superfluous to give
rules to one who knows, *praecepta dare scienti supervacuum est*" (Seneca *Epistles*
94.11).[10] It would seem to follow that rules are "intended for the guidance of
the *prokoptontes* who had not the training, opportunity, or brain for the *logos*-
philosophy to be true *sapientes*."[11]

Since men apply themselves to the task of attaining perfection with varying
degrees of concentration, most if not all men fall into this category. Yet some
prokoptontes are closer to the *summum bonum* than others:

Just as the man immediately below the surface, though in danger of drown-
ing, is in fact nearer to safety than the wretch lying on the bottom, so the
prokoptōn is nearer to virtue, in the sense that, if he continues along his present path, he will eventually become virtuous, even though he is still utterly
vicious.[12]

The classification *prokoptontes* then covers a multitude of sins, both literally and
figuratively. For the Stoic, it was broad enough to include what we might
regard as the saint as well as the sinner. Thus Posidonius "placed Socrates
among the *prokoptontes* as Zeno had already set Plato."[13] But the essential difference between a Plato and a person like the tyrant Dionysius was that the
former could be hopeful and the latter "might as well despair of wisdom."[14]
The point here, echoes of which we find in Philo, is that clear, undisputed
cases of *sophoi* are very rare indeed. By and large, mankind is composed of
men struggling to attain the distant heights of the sage.[15]

Philo's classification of men, while containing some familiar Stoic themes,
also has some features which do not have obvious Stoic sources. The first passage to consider is *Heres* 45–46:

Now there are three kinds of life, one looking Godwards, another looking
to created things, another on the border-line, a mixture of the other two.
The God-regarding life has never come down to us, nor submitted to the
constraints of the body. The life that looks to creation has never risen at all

nor sought to rise, but makes its lair in the recesses of Hades and rejoices in a form of living, which is not worth the pains. It is the mixed life, which often drawn on by those of the higher line is possessed and inspired by God, though often pulled back by the worse it reverses its course.

This account seems to be reasonably straightforward. Of the three types of men inhabiting Philo's world, the highest category is composed of immaterial beings, or as Wolfson calls them, "unbodied souls or angels."[16] Immediately beneath them are men of mixed nature. Colson correctly identified them with "the ordinary virtuous man (*ho prokoptōn*)."[17] Lower still is a class of evil men.

In a second passage (from *Legum Allegoria*) the tripartite division remains. This time each class of mankind is considered in relation to its need for rules. In the highest category is an immaterial being who is "created after His image and after the original idea."[18] He is contrasted with Adam, the ordinary man. As in the case of the Stoic sage, the immaterial man does not need external rules, for he possesses virtue instinctively.[19] Adam, on the other hand, is in need of instruction. Philo's formulation of the distinction is as follows:

> Now it is to this being [Adam], and not to the being created after His image and after the original idea, that God gives the command. For the latter, even without urging, possesses virtue instinctively; but the former, independently of instruction, could have no part in wisdom. There is a difference between these three—injunction, prohibition, command accompanied by exhortation. For prohibition deals with wrongdoings and is addressed to the bad man, injunction concerns duties rightly done, and exhortation is addressed to the neutral man (*pros ton meson*), the man who is neither bad nor good (*ton mēte phaulon mēte spoudaion*): for he is neither sinning, to lead anyone to forbid him, nor is he so doing right as right reason enjoins, but has need of exhortation, which teaches him to refrain from evil things, and incites him to aim at things noble. There is no need, then, to give injunctions or prohibitions or exhortations to the perfect man formed after the (Divine) image . . . (*LA* i.92–94).

The correspondences between these passages now may be seen in parallel columns.

LA i.92–94	*Heres* 45–46
1. *spoudaios*	
is generic man of *Opif.* 69 ff.	looks toward God
possesses virtue instinctively	has never come down to us
is perfect	has not submitted to the body
(parallel to Stoic sage)	(unbodied souls or angels, according to Wolfson)

2. *mesos*

is neutral man, neither bad nor good	leads mixed life: can look toward God, or alternatively, toward created things
is in need of instruction	
profits from instruction, exhortation	border-line, but does seek to rise
(parallel to Stoic progressive man)	(*prokoptōn,* according to Colson)

3. *phaulos*

is bad man	looks only toward created things
profits only from prohibitions	does not seek to rise
cannot be taught	

From these two passages we might conclude that Philo's classification of mankind is static. The *phaulos* does not seek to rise; the *prokoptōn* might aspire upwards, but is often pulled down; and angels are angels. In *Gig.* 60–63, however, Philo again makes a tripartite distinction between men. Since he does not use the terminology noted earlier, we should first satisfy ourselves that Philo is making the same distinctions as before, albeit in different words. Then we shall determine the differences.

> Some men are earth-born, some heaven-born, and some God-born. The earth-born are those who take the pleasures of the body for their quarry, who make it their practice to indulge in them and enjoy them and provide the means by which each of them may be promoted. The heaven-born are the votaries of the arts (*technitai*) and of knowledge, the lovers of learning. For the heavenly element in us is the mind, as the heavenly beings are each of them a mind. And it is the mind which pursues the learning of the schools (*ta enkyklia*) and the other arts one and all. . . . But the men of God are priests and prophets who have refused to accept membership in the commonwealth of the world and to become citizens therein, but have risen wholly above the sphere of sense-perception and have been translated into the world of the intelligible and dwell there registered as freemen of the commonwealth of Ideas (*ideōn politeia*), which are imperishable and incorporeal.
>
> Thus Abraham, while he sojourned in the land of the Chaldaeans— sojourned, that is, in mere opinion (*doxē*)—and with his name as yet unchanged from Abram, was a "man of heaven" (*anthrōpos ouranou*). . . . But when he has risen to a better state and the time is at hand that his name should be changed, he becomes a man of God (*anthrōpos theou*) . . . (*Gig.* 60–63).

The terms "man of God," "man of heaven," and "man of earth" clearly correspond to the categories (1), (2), and (3) as we have already depicted them.[20] But here, instead of a static set of classifications, there is movement, particularly from category (2) to (1). Philo gives as an example of such movement the case of Abraham who begins his life as Abram, an ordinary man in the progressive class. He becomes a "man of God" while still subject to the constraints of the body. Priests and prophets, mentioned in *Gig.* 61, also are men of flesh and blood. There is no suggestion here that these members of the highest category are generic men, unbodied souls, or angels. What is missing from the account based on *LA* i.92–95 and *Heres* 45–46, then, is precisely this aspect of mobility.[21]

Of equal interest in *Gig.* 60–63 is the fact that men in the middle category are virtually *defined* by their study of the encyclia. Abraham, the prototype of the man of heaven, is not the only member of this class who turns to encyclical studies as a means of progressing.[22] Indeed, as we shall see, the encyclia play a critical role in the lives of all ordinary men—both those fortunate enough to become "men of God" and those who live out their lives on the level at which they began.

Since virtue and knowledge are so closely linked in Philo's mind, it should come as no surprise that Philo makes a tripartite division again—this one based on ethical criteria. In *QG* iv.243, Philo distinguishes three moral spheres. On the extremes are the regions of virtue and wickedness; in the middle is "a land in which the Chaldaeans and Babylonians dwell . . . which is progress and improvement [Marcus' reconstruction: *prokopē kai beltiōsis*], (that is) a path leading to felicity."[23] We shall now discuss each of these spheres and the types of men which inhabit them.

2. Individual Classes of Men

God-born Men. From the passages we have already examined, the highest class of men would seem to consist of unbodied souls, angels, and human beings of an extraordinary nature. To be more precise about the upper reaches of this class, we should consider this Philonic passage:

> The air is the abode of incorporeal souls, since it seemed good to their Maker to fill all parts of the universe with living beings. . . . Accordingly let no one take away nature at its best, as it is in living creatures, from the best of earth's elements, air: for so far is air from being alone of all things untenanted, that like a city it has a goodly population, its citizens being imperishable and immortal souls equal in number to the stars (*Som.* i.135–37).

If we read further (until section 143), it becomes clear that the cosmos is filled with elevated beings of different sorts.[24] Philo seems to apply the principle of plenitude, with the result that his universe is replete with incorporeal God-born beings.[25]

Immediately beneath the incorporeal beings, there are *sophoi* who seem to partake of both the immaterial and the material world. *Heres* 84 introduces this group:

> When the mind is ministering to God in purity, it is not human, but divine. But when it ministers to aught that is human, it turns its course and descending from heaven, or rather falling to earth, comes forth even though his body still remains within.

Commenting on *Heres* 84, Holladay says, "the soul of *ho sophos* is not necessarily confined to somatic existence, in spite of its attachment to *sōma* (*sema*)."[26] In another passage concerning the sagacious man, Philo makes the point in a different way: "Though there be few such upon earth, in heaven vast is their number" (*Mut.* 256).[27] There are *sophoi*, then, on all levels of the spiritual world. Some of these *sophoi* are primarily immaterial by nature; others are more firmly fixed in *this* world. Our concern lies primarily with the latter, for their experience in coming to knowledge of God is of relevance to man.

In order to place the sage within a pedagogical context, it is actually necessary to distinguish between two types of sages. Both are on the material end of the scale of *sophoi*; in short, they are not angels. But both are capable of rising to "minister to God in purity." The two types of *sophoi* to which I allude are (i) true men of God who are born as such and (ii) men like Abram/Abraham who are born as men of heaven, but rise by diligence to take their places among the men of God.

(i) *True men of God: sages by birth.* L. K. K. Dey has compiled a list of the terms which may be applied to beings in the highest category: viz., *teleios, ho kat' eikona, spoudaios, to tēs pros theon zōēs genos, anthrōpoi theou*.[28] Some of these terms are familiar to us from Stoic usage. One appellation, not mentioned by Dey, is *ho echōn ton klēron* (*Sob.* 56). This phrase, Tsekourakis notes, "does not seem to fit the Stoic teaching." He continues further:

> The word *klēros* (a lot, that which is assigned by lot, a legacy) cannot find a very suitable place in the ethics of the Early Stoa, whether it means "a lot" deriving from fortune or from god. . . . The Early Stoics believed that it was not god who bestowed virtue and wisdom on men.[29]

Herein lies a significant point of departure between the Stoic concept of the sage and that of Philo. Despite certain similarities in terminology and conception, for Philo it was God who bestowed wisdom on those born into the highest category. For example, Isaac, who was perfect by nature, was overseen by God from the moment of conception.[30] The grace of God, then, is an essential element in the original constitution of the sage.[31]

The most illustrious members of the highest class seem to have been *nomoi empsychoi*: that is, according to Goodenough, "unwritten representations of God's revealed nature and will."[32] The attribute may be seen in Abraham in his depiction as a fully developed sage:

> Abraham, then, filled with zeal for piety, the highest and greatest of virtues, was eager to follow God and to be obedient to His commands; understanding by commands not only those conveyed in speech and writing but also those made manifest by nature with clearer signs. . . . For anyone who contemplates the order in nature and the constitution enjoyed by the world-city . . . needs no speaker to teach him to practise a law-abiding and peaceful life . . . (*Abr.* 60–61).

Both Isaac and Moses have strong claims to being *nomoi empsychoi*. Isaac was born perfect; and Moses, as Lawgiver, was "the reasonable and living impersonation of law" (*Mos.* i.162, *nomos empsychos te kai logikos*).[33] But as we have already noted in discussing *LA* i.92–95, even the more humble beings who fill the ranks of the sages have no need for external rules.

Since we have mentioned Philonic exemplars, we should return to Moses, who is the most perfect of the sages.[34] Not only is Moses depicted as a *sophos*; he is also portrayed as the *philos theou*.[35] For a fuller appreciation of Moses as the God-born man we could do no better than to consider *Sac.* 8–9.[36]

> [Lacuna]. . . . There are still others, whom God has advanced even higher, and has trained them to soar above species and genus alike (*eidē* . . . *kai genē*) and stationed them beside himself. Such is Moses to whom He says "stand here with Me" (Deut. v. 31). . . . Thus you may learn that God prizes the Wise Man (*ton sophon*) as the world, for that same Word, by which He made the universe, is that by which He draws the perfect man (*ton teleion*) from things earthly to Himself. And even when He sent him as a loan to the earthly sphere and suffered him to dwell therein, He gifted him with no ordinary excellence, such as that which kings and rulers have, wherewith to hold sway and sovereignty over the passions of the soul, but He appointed him as god (*theon*), placing all the bodily region and the mind which rules it in subjection and slavery to him.

This passage, while helping us to see the unique qualities of the sage *par excellence,* raises a problem which must be faced squarely. Did Moses sin? Let us suppose that, as *Sac.* 9 indicates, Moses held sway over the passions much more effectively than any other man.[37] Nevertheless, did he still err? No easy answer to this question is possible. We may agree, with Holladay,[38] that *De Vita Mosis* tends to present Moses in a more blameless light than the Biblical narrative does. (To expect anything else from a clearly apologetic work would be mistaken.) In an effort to restore a proper balance, Holladay correctly notes that any being in Philo's universe, simply by virtue of being *created,* is liable to sin.[39] So where does this leave Moses? Wolfson leaves the issue unresolved,[40] and Holladay follows suit.[41]

In my opinion, *Det.* 161f. provides some indication of Philo's position on the sinlessness of Moses:

> And so it is said in the Holy Books: "I give you as god to Pharaoh" (Ex. 7:1). . . . What then is to be deduced from these observations? This: the wise man is said to be "god" of the fool, while in reality he is not a god at all. . . . But when, however, the wise man is set side-by-side with the Existent One, he will be discovered to be a man of God (*anthrōpos . . . theou*); but, by contrast, when he is set side-by-side with a fool, one can form an *opinion* and *imagine* that he is a god, though in actual fact he is really not, even then.[42]

As we have seen elsewhere,[43] Philo often writes from two opposing points of view. The fool, the newcomer to Judaism, or the unsophisticated may opine—and here Philo deliberately uses the language of "seeming"—that Moses is sinless. From their limited perspectives, this appears to be the case. As an exemplar for men of simple faith, Moses may be thought perfect. The reality, however, is different: God (insofar as philosophers can understand God's vision) sees Moses merely as an *anthrōpos theou,* a technical term equivalent to "sage." Sages, at least in the eyes of God, are mortal; their moral lapses, inevitable. As Philo writes in *QG* iv.77, "It is not wide of the mark to say that the soul of the wise man, having a body that is inanimate and heavy, like a bronze statue, is always carrying a corpse." I believe this answers the question of "sinlessness" among Philo's sages (Moses not excepted) as graphically and definitively as we might hope.

(ii) *Men of heaven who become sages.* In *Gig.* 61, Philo mentions that "men of God are priests and prophets who . . . have risen wholly above the sphere of sense-perception. . . ." These were originally men of heaven. Their prototype, the lowest level within the category of *sophoi,* is Abraham. They were able to ascend by a proper combination of instruction, nature, and practice.[44] The fact that Philo mentions prophets here is, in itself, significant because within the Philonic framework virtually any refined, wise, and just man is "capable of attaining prophecy."[45] Thus we may rest assured that the circle of *sophoi* is not an exclusive one and, while there are few such men on earth, nothing in principle prevents there being more.

In our discussion of the sage it would be well to cite a passage in which Philo compares him with the ordinary man in the "heaven-born" category.[46] The passage is based upon Deut. 5.5, "And I stood between the Lord and you." Philo claims that scripture here

. . . does not mean that he stood firm upon his feet, but wishes to indicate that the mind of the Sage (*sophou*), released from storms and wars, with calm still weather and profound peace around it, is superior to men, but less than God. For the human mind of the common sort shakes and swirls under the force of chance events, while the other, in virtue of its blessedness and felicity, is exempt from evil. The good man [i.e., the sage] indeed is on the border-line, so that we may say, quite properly, that he is neither God nor man, but bounded at either end by the two, by mortality because of his manhood, by incorruption because of his virtue (*Som.* ii.229–30).

Heaven-born Men. We now move down into the world of "storms and wars" to examine the ordinary man who lives under the sway of contrary impulses. Our initial characterization of the heaven-born man is taken from *Som.* ii.234–35, a continuation of the passage quoted above. The contrast is clear in Philo's mind;[47] unlike the *sophoi* who are "on the border-line between the uncreated and the perishing form of being [i.e., the material world],"

> the man who is on the path of progress (*prokoptonta*) is placed by him in the region between the living and the dead, meaning by the former those who have wisdom for their life-mate and by the latter those who rejoice in folly. . . . For the man of progress (*ho prokoptōn*) does not rank either among those dead to the life of virtue, since his desires aspire to moral excellence, nor yet among those who live in supreme and perfect happiness, since he still falls short of the consummation, but is in touch with both.

The most obvious instance of a heaven-born man is Abram.[48] He is not, however, the most typical, for unlike the majority of his confreres, Abram eventually transcends the class into which he was born. Before discussing Bezalel, who is more representative of the class of heaven-born men, let us take note of the primary terms by which Philo refers to this group. They are, according to Dey, *mesos, nēpios, Adam, gēinos nous, miktos, peplasmenos, prokoptōn, methorios,* and *anthrōpoi ouranou*.[49] What is apparent in this list is the median quality of heaven-born men. Men in this class are mid-stream in terms of learning,[50] ethics, and spiritual development. Philo says, for instance, that "a soul, while making gradual progress (*prokoptousa*), is not yet capable of availing itself of Wisdom's untempered draught, but such a soul is not prevented from staying hard by her" (*Fug.* 202). We are dealing then with unsophisticated, ordinary men. Their goal of Wisdom, however, is not necessarily beyond their grasp.

The heaven-born man, we have remarked before, is a man of progress.[51] "Progress" in the context which will interest us does not simply mean that a man of heaven should try to emulate Abram by advancing to the level of a *sophos*. It also means that he can take a more modest course by following the path of Bezalel, as the ensuing quotations (followed by a more extended analysis in Chapter 4) should make clear.

There are essentially two paths by which men reach the heights in Philo. These paths are expounded in two passages which must be cited at length. In the first passage, Philo has been talking about knowledge of the existence of God; he continues,

> Struck with admiration and astonishment they arrived at a conception according with what they beheld, that surely all these beauties and this transcendent order has not come into being automatically but by the handiwork of an architect and world maker. . . .
>
> These no doubt are truly admirable persons and superior to the other classes. They have . . . advanced from down to up by a sort of heavenly ladder and by reason and reflection happily inferred the Creator from His works. But those, if such there be, who have had the power to apprehend Him through Himself without the co-operation of any reasoning process to lead them to the sight, must be recorded as holy and genuine worshippers and friends of God in very truth. . . .
>
> And this knowledge he has gained not from any other source, not from things on earth or things in Heaven . . . but at the summons of Him alone who has willed to reveal His existence as a person to the suppliant (*Praem.* 42–44).

The second passage speaks of those who come to know God from the harmony of the world and its constituent parts. Such men, Philo says,

> who . . . base their reasoning on what is before their eyes, apprehend God by means of a shadow cast, discerning the Artificer by means of His works. There is a mind more perfect and more thoroughly cleansed, which has undergone initiation into the great mysteries, a mind which gains its knowledge of the First Cause not from created things, as one may learn the substance from the shadow, but lifting its eyes above and beyond creation obtains a clear vision of the uncreated One, so as from Him to apprehend both Himself and His shadow. . . . The mind of which I speak is Moses who says, "Manifest Thyself to me, let me see Thee that I may know Thee" (Exod. xxxiii. 13); 'for I would not that Thou shouldst be manifested to me by means of heaven or earth or water or air or any created thing at all, nor would I find the reflection of Thy being in aught else than in Thee Who art God, for the reflections in created things are dissolved, but those in the Uncreate will continue abiding and sure and eternal.' This is why God hath expressly called Moses and why He spake to Him. Bezalel also He hath expressly called, but not in like manner. One receives the clear vision of God directly from the First Cause Himself. The other discerns the Artificer, as it were from a shadow, from created things by virtue of a process of reasoning (*LA* iii.99–102).

Correlating these passages, we find a revealing dichotomy. There are those who have a positive orientation toward the created world, learn with the faculty of sight by a process of reasoning, and are instructed by something outside of themselves, namely, the Cosmos; their advance is "from down to up" (*Praem.* 43). With a trace of hesitancy, Philo then describes those who arrive at the highest knowledge by another path. While Philo does not explicitly say that these "friends of God" have a negative orientation toward the created world, they have no need for the world apprehended by the senses. Attuned to the invisible, these men do not have to rely on the reasoning process. Rather, they attain knowledge by intuition and divine grace.[52]

Wolfson is aware of the divisions noted here. He correctly delineates the two fundamental methods of arriving at knowledge of the existence of God: (i) the indirect method, whereby "knowledge of nature is gathered slowly and painstakingly by observation and experience, and the proof for the existence of God is derived, again, slowly, syllogistically, from premise through premise to conclusion" and (ii) the direct method, whereby "knowledge of nature is showered upon a person suddenly by divine revelation, and similarly the proof of the existence of God derived therefrom is flashed upon a person's mind suddenly, again by divine revelation."[53] Wolfson sees these distinctions essentially in terms of two kinds of knowledge of the mind.[54] But Philo is not only describing minds; he is also presenting two real pedagogical and theological models according to which men can attain knowledge of God. Moses and Bezalel, as elsewhere, are prototypes by which Philo indicates to his readers two different paths—that of the sage and that of the progressive man, respectively.[55] We shall discuss the ascents of these two types of men in detail in the following chapter. Meanwhile, it is appropriate to cite another passage in which Philo contrasts them.

> Moses, the keeper and guardian of the mysteries of the Existent One, will be one called above; for it is said in the Book of Leviticus, "He called Moses up above" (Lev. i.1). One called up above will Bezalel also be, held worthy of a place in the second rank. For him also does God call up above for the construction and overseeing of the sacred works (Exod. xxxi.2ff.). But while Bezalel shall carry off the lower honours conferred by the call above, Moses the all-wise shall bear away the primary honours. For the former fashions the shadows, just as painters do. . . . Moses on the other hand obtained the office of producing not shadows but the actual archetype of the several objects (*Plant.* 26–27).[56]

When a man like Bezalel learns from the created world he is doing what the student of the encyclia does. If, by chance, he is able to leap forward to the level of a sage, that should be regarded as his good fortune, "unforeseen and unhoped for" (*Sac.* 78).[57] In the normal course of events, an ordinary man should not expect this much. In *Som.* ii.232–33, Philo describes a mind "mastered by the love of the divine." This mind, after an arduous struggle, "forgets all else, forgets itself, and fixes its thoughts and memories on Him alone Whose attendant and servant it is. . . ." But, continues Philo, "when the inspiration is stayed, and the strong yearning abates, it hastens back from the divine and becomes a man and meets the human interests which lay in the vestibule ready to seize upon it, should it but shew its face for a moment from within." In this account, we see a vivid picture of a man of progress who is successful in rising to the level of a sage. What is particularly interesting, though, is Philo's admission of the transitory nature of his achievement, an admission which is paralleled by Philo's well-known autobiographical statement of *Spec.* iii.1–6. From these two passages, we might reasonably conclude that Philo thinks of most men (himself included) as heaven-born. Among these men there are individuals who can lift themselves heavenward without risking shipwreck. Yet, with deep regret, Philo seems to look at these moments of divine insight as the exceptions for men who ordinarily live on a lower level. It is only appropriate, then, that the human soul should be pictured (in *Som.* i.146–47) on Jacob's ladder, where his descent is considered as inevitable as his ascent is desirable. The result, of course, is that the presence of God cannot long remain with most people. As Philo says in *Gig.* 53,

> Thus it is that in the many (*tois pollois*), those, that is, who have set before them many ends in life, the divine spirit does not abide, even though it sojourn there for a while.[58]

Earth-born Men. The most striking analogy used to describe earth-born men[59] is a culinary one. Philo has been discussing prophets, those who truly see: i.e., God-born men. Then he turns to the opposite extreme.

> But the others even if they do ever open their eyes have bent them earthwards; they pursue the things of earth and their conversation is with the dwellers in Hades. The one extends his vision to the ether and the revolutions of the heaven; he has been trained also to look stedfastly for the manna, which is the word of God, the heavenly incorruptible food of the soul which delights in the vision. But the others see but the onions and the garlic, which give great pain and trouble to their eyes and make them close, or the other ill-smelling things, the leeks and dead fishes, which are food proper to Egypt . . . (*Heres* 78–79).[60]

Elsewhere the image changes and, instead of associating earth-born men with ill-smelling foods, Philo accuses them of seeking only pleasures of the body. With their hedonistic proclivities, *phauloi* do not have the inclination or the mental discipline even to study God's works in the world, to say nothing of drawing theological conclusions from their observations.[61] *Phauloi* are very similar to, if not identical with, the individuals mentioned in *Decal.* 59, about whom Philo says:

Incapacity for instruction or indifference to learning prevents them from knowing the truly Existent because they suppose that there is no invisible and conceptual cause outside what the senses perceive. . . .

If there is a prototype of the earth-born man it is, as Knox correctly points out, Nimrod.[62] *Gig.* 65, which makes this identification explicit, is worth citing in full not only because it rounds out our picture of this class of mankind, but also because it leads us naturally to our consideration of free will.

> But the sons of earth (*hoi de gēs paides*) have turned the steps of the mind out of the path of reason and transmuted it into the lifeless and inert nature of the flesh. . . . Thus they have debased the coin of truest metal and deserted from their post, left a place that was better for a worse, a place amid their own people for a place amid their foes. It was Nimrod who began this desertion. For the lawgiver says "he began to be a giant on the earth" (Gen. x.8), and his name means "desertion."

3. Free Will and Human Choice

In a discussion of the subject of free will as it relates to Philonic education, *Gig.* 65 is a significant passage. Many of Philo's references to earth-born men or *phauloi* are invective.[63] But *Gig.* 65 gives us a fuller picture of the career of a man of earth. In it Philo clearly says that Nimrod, the prototype, deserted his post. From this hint and the remainder of the passage, we may infer that at least some earth-born men were originally endowed with reason and that they willingly chose to abandon this legacy. Nimrod, we are told, was once a man of heaven, in which case his constitution would not have differed from that of Bezalel. Yet the former descended, while the latter came to know God by means of his works. These considerations lead us to the conclusion that there is an element of free will within Philo's system.

Unfortunately the issue of free will is not so straightforward as my opening remarks would indicate. First of all, there can be no progress without the active aid of God.[64] To speak in anthropomorphic terms, only God knows the criteria according to which men are judged worthy of his grace.[65] Human attempts to fathom God's will are doomed to failure, as are all efforts to rise beyond one's limit.[66] It would seem that the less gifted the individual (at the start), the less successful he will be in any endeavor to lift himself. As Philo says in *QG* iv.33, "The divine powers accept the perfect man, while to the imperfect man they hardly ever come."[67] Yet it was God, through his powers, who made this man perfect and that one imperfect.[68]

Philo approached the subject of what education could or could not accomplish with caution. Since God's will is decisive in determining man's nature and since one's nature sets certain limits to human development, education itself is not conclusive. For instance, education cannot transform a fool into a sage. But Philo believed, as did the Stoics, that ordinary men could make moral progress and that virtue could be taught.[69] Within these limitations, education plays a positive role in human life.

If we may apply these principles to the classes of men as set forth in *Heres* 45–46 and *LA* i.92–94, it is obvious that the men at the two extremes are not at liberty to change their lots in life. On the one hand, there are God-regarding men who by nature act in harmony with the world-order. Although, as humans, they might sin, their sins do not change their station in life. (Nor do these sins appear particularly heinous to ordinary mortals.) Their personal freedom consists only in slight deviations from inborn perfection. At the other extreme, there is "the life that looks to creation." This type of man is sunk in Hades, "has never risen at all nor sought to rise." His freedom would seem to consist in choosing between onion and garlic. The true sage, having been released from the turmoil of the passions, is not subject to evil temptation; the *phaulos*, however, cannot resist it. The opposition of the two extremes is quite explicit, as we see in *Immut.* 143:

> For wisdom is a straight high road, and it is when the mind's course is guided along that road that it reaches the goal which is the recognition and knowledge of God. Every comrade of the flesh hates and rejects this path and seeks to corrupt it. For there are no two things so utterly opposed as knowledge and pleasure of the flesh.[70]

Human choices lie in the middle ground. We may consider, then, three different paths, all of which begin with men of heaven: that of Abraham who became a sage, that of Bezalel who stayed at his post and came to know God through the created world, and that of Nimrod who fell into the lowest class by abandoning the path of reason.[71] From the passages examined above, I would conclude that Nimrod might have chosen to live the life of Bezalel; Bezalel, however, probably could not have elected to live the life of Abram/Abraham. This, then, is the spectrum of human life within which it is possible to alter one's condition. Obviously Philo was not thinking in terms of a concept of absolute free will when he charted these courses.[72]

Ideally a man takes the path which corresponds most closely to his position in Philo's hierarchy of men.

> Both forms of virtue, one where the teacher is another, one where the teacher and learner are the same, will be open to human kind. And where man is weak he will claim the former, where he is strong the latter which comes ready to his hands (*Mut.* 263).[73]

Here the weaker or ordinary man proceeds by means of instruction from without; this course is inferior to being *autodidaktos*. Philo often speaks of the path on which progressive men find themselves as "second best." Yet he does not view this alternative pejoratively, for "there is in it an element of a way of thinking such as God approves" (*Abr.* 123).[74] To men of limited endowment, the second-best voyage is the only way of progressing, and consequently, Philo seems to speak of it with compassion:

> If . . . a man is absolutely incapable of holding intercourse with the understanding by itself, he wins in sense-perception a second-best refuge. . . . For those who have failed to make a good voyage under the sails of the sovereign mind can always fall back upon the oars of sense-perception (*Som.* i.44).

By virtue of their capacities, ordinary men are not ill-advised when they are told to stay within the bounds of what they, as men of "mixed" natures, may appropriately learn. "All such as are enamoured of things too great for their nature will be convicted of foolishness, since every effort beyond our strength breaks down through over-violent straining" (*Fug.* 146). Elsewhere the same sentiment is repeated, perhaps even more forcefully. Having warned men of an "excess of boldness," Philo writes:

> Loss is entailed by all movement that is not under Divine direction, and it is better to stay where we are, roaming, with the bulk of mankind, through this mortal life, rather than to lift ourselves heavenward and incur shipwreck as impostors (*Mig.* 171).[75]

Since the second-best path *is* the way of the encyclical studies, we should not be surprised to find the path described in the same terms as the encyclia were.[76] This is evident in *Spec.* i.36–40:

> Nothing is better than to search for the true God, even if the discovery of Him eludes human capacity, since the very wish to learn, if earnestly entertained, produces untold joys and pleasures. We have the testimony of those who have not taken a mere sip of philosophy but have feasted more abundantly on its reasonings and conclusions. For with them the reason soars away from earth into the heights, travels through the upper air and accompanies the revolutions of the sun and moon and the whole heaven and in its desire to see all that is there finds its powers of sight blurred, for so pure and vast is the radiance that pours therefrom that the soul's eye is dizzied by the flashing of the rays. Yet it does not therefore faintheartedly give up the task, but with purpose unsubdued presses onwards to such contemplation as is possible, like the athlete who strives for the second prize since he has been disappointed of the first. Now second to the true vision stands conjecture and theorizing (*eikasia kai stochasmos*) and all that can be brought into the category of reasonable probability. . . . Though the clear vision of God as He really is is denied us, we ought not to relinquish the quest. For the very seeking, even without finding, is felicity in itself. . . .

The description of the soul soaring away from the earth, which could apply to Moses, Isaac, Abraham, or any other true sage, reflects the mystic side of Philo's thought. I should like to focus, however, on the path not taken by the *sophos*. Again we note that Philo does not disparage either the inferior quest or the conjectures it necessarily produces. One possible reason for Philo's receptivity to the second-best path is his awareness that even the most virtuous of ordinary men cannot be *certain* of rising to the level of a sage. Be that as it may, within the second-best category we find Philo's own reflections on the realities of the human condition.

4. Imitation of Moses, Isaac, and Abraham[77]

From our discussion of the types of mankind, we can conclude that there are three praiseworthy patterns of life. They may be summarized in ascending order as follows:

(1) the man of heaven who, like Bezalel, keeps within the limitations of his endowment and yet comes to know God,
(2) the man of heaven who, like Abram, transcends his original endowment and becomes a sage, and
(3) the man of God who, like Moses or Isaac, is a perfect sage from the start.

While most ordinary men probably fall into the first-mentioned category, Philo holds up both the second and third possibilities as ideals worthy of emulation.[78] To be sure, they are ideals in different senses. Abraham is a model for the *acquisition* of virtue. Neither Moses nor Isaac is a model of this sort because, as perfect beings, virtue came to them by nature. Nevertheless, they are supreme models for the *activity* of virtue, for the activity of leading a virtuous life.

Despite their differences, Moses, Isaac, and Abraham have one thing in common: they are at the center of an educational system which places a premium on imitation.[79] For instance, in the opening paragraphs of *De Abrahamo,* Philo writes:

Let us postpone consideration of particular laws, which are, so to speak, copies, and examine first those which are more general and may be called the originals of those copies. These are such men as lived good and blameless lives, whose virtues stand permanently recorded in the most holy scriptures, not merely to sound their praises but for the instruction of the reader and as an inducement to him to aspire to the same. . . (*Abr.* 3-4).[80]

Two types of men are advanced as models for imitation: first the perfect man, then the progressive man who succeeds in becoming a sage. We shall consider them after saying a few words about the source of Philo's prototypes.

Despite Philo's liberal use of Biblical texts for a multitude of purposes, he clearly distinguishes between the historical part of the Bible and that having to do with commands and prohibitions (the law). The historical part of the Bible is then subdivided again:

> One division of the historical side deals with the creation of the world, the other with particular persons, and this last partly with the punishment of the impious, partly with the honouring of the just (*Mos.* ii.47).

Our interest here lies with particular persons, their rewards and punishments. In contrast with ordinary writers, Moses (whom Philo took to be the author of the Torah[81]) does not "make it his business to leave behind for posterity records of ancient deeds for the pleasant but unimproving entertainment which they give. . ." (*ibid.,* 48). On the contrary, Moses transcends ordinary history, thereby achieving, in a sense, the goal of *true* history, moral instruction through positive example:

> The information that Terah left the land of Chaldaea and migrated to Haran . . . is given us not with the object that we may learn as from a writer of history, that certain people became emigrants, leaving the land of their ancestors . . . but that a lesson well suited to man and of great service to human life may not be neglected (*Som.* i.52).

Having adopted the didactic value of Scripture as primary, Philo makes the issue of whether an "event" in the Bible actually happened, as recorded, secondary.[82] Since the questions of "fact" are subordinated in this way to the deeper truths which lie hidden in Scripture, Philo can even dismiss reports which the Bible contains:

> When . . . you hear of Hagar as afflicted or evil-entreated by Sarah, do not suppose that you have here one of the usual accompaniments of women's jealousy. It is not women that are spoken of here; it is minds. . . (*Cong.* 180).

But precisely because stories from Scripture contain hidden truths, the Bible is the only reliable source for finding exemplars for human behavior.[83]

Moses and Isaac as Models. Several passages make specific reference to the fact that one should imitate Moses. For instance in *Mos.* i.158–59, Philo writes:

> And thus, leading the way into the middle (*eis meson proagagōn*), [Moses] set up himself and his own life as a well-wrought picture, a piece of work most beautiful and godlike, a model (*paradeigma*) for those willing to copy it. Happy are they who imprint, or strive to imprint, that image in their souls.[84]

And again in *Virt.* 51, we read that Moses "used to incite and train all his subjects to fellowship, setting before them the monument of his own life like an original design to be their beautiful model." The imitation of Moses, then, is put forward as an ideal human activity.[85]

We should have no illusions about the proximity of Moses to the ordinary man or the ability of that man to model his life after Moses'.[86] Philo presents Moses as the highest example of human perfection. Indeed he lives on a plane which far transcends that of Abraham:

> Mark the advance to improvement made by the soul that has an insatiable desire to be filled with things that are beautiful, and the unlimited wealth of God, which has given as starting-points to others the goals reached by those before them. For the limit of the knowledge attained by Seth became the starting-point of righteous Noah; while Abraham begins his education with the consummation of Noah's; and the highest point of wisdom reached by Abraham is the initial course in Moses' training (*Post.* 174).

For the purposes of our study, it is significant that the divine Lawgiver is pictured as having devoted himself to the encyclia:

> Arithmetic, geometry, the lore of metre, rhythm and harmony, and the whole subject of music . . . were imparted to him by learned Egyptians. . . . He had Greeks to teach him the rest of the regular school course (*enkyklion paideian*), and the inhabitants of the neighbouring countries for Assyrian letters and the Chaldaean science of the heavenly bodies (*tēn tōn ouraniōn Chaldaikēn epistēmēn, Mos.* i.23).

The very transcendence of Moses' position elicited a surprised response from Marcus, who apparently found it incongruous for Moses to demean himself with ordinary studies.[87] Goodenough's reaction to the same phenomenon was to assert that Moses' "encyclical studies mean nothing to him."[88] The question, however, is not what the encyclia meant to Moses, but rather what they could mean to someone modeling his life after the Lawgiver. Especially if we assume that *De Vita Mosis* is an apologetic work, there is every reason for Philo to elaborate any points of contact between the experience of his audience and that of his protagonist. One of these points would be encyclical education.

Moses, the self-taught, rather quickly transcends the encyclical studies.[89] As a model for the *activity* of virtue, he is very similar to Isaac. Both are perfect by nature, but to an ordinary man Isaac might appear more distant than Moses. For there is a certain supraterrestrial quality about Philo's depiction of Isaac. That quality might stem from the suggestion of Isaac's divine paternity,[90] or from the fact that he never descended into the mundane world (even to study the encyclia), or possibly from statements to the effect that he was "not a man, but a most pure thought" (*Fug.* 167). In view of these considerations, it is no wonder that Leisegang should question whether Isaac actually was a man of flesh and blood.[91]

One other facet of Isaac's personality deserves mention and that is his representation of "nature" in the educational triad of learning, nature, and practice.[92] Isaac, by his very being, reminds the aspiring student that one's natural endowment is an essential ingredient of all progress.

Abraham as Model. Abraham is a model for the *acquisition* of virtue. We have already seen in *Gig.* 60–63 that this patriarch began his life in a foreign land which Philo equates with *doxa* and alien doctrines. Abraham's primary appeal, then, is to the proselyte who initially has no relation to monotheism. The connection between Abraham and the potential convert seems to have been a natural one, for Philo was not the only Hellenistic Jewish author to use Abram, the Chaldaean, as a link between Judaism and paganism.[93] Indeed Mayer has argued that Abraham was the main figure in a missionary literature.[94] Philo is simply participating in a well-established tradition when he holds Abraham up for imitation by those uninitiated into the faith. But Abraham's appeal does not end with the proselyte. Any ordinary Jew (or man of heaven) who wished to make spiritual progress would turn to Abraham as to a beacon. For, unlike Moses and Isaac, Abram had to be "weaned from falsehood,"[95] and the number of men who could identify with his migration is legion. Sandmel, whose depiction of Abraham touches on all aspects of the patriarch's career in Philo, takes the issue we have been discussing one step further: Sandmel argues that Philo applied various lessons, which he inferred from the life of Abraham, to his own personal life.[96]

Perhaps the clearest lesson which ordinary men are meant to draw from the life of Abraham is that they should study the encyclia. As we have already noted, studying the encyclia does not guarantee entry to the realm of the *sophoi*. Even if a student masters the encyclical disciplines, he is not necessarily able to transcend the world of sense-perception. It is safe to say, however, that a man of heaven who models his life after Abraham will do no worse than Bezalel did in apprehending God from his works in the world. This second-best voyage, essentially, is the hope which the figure of Abraham holds out to his devotees. It is a path which should console both the proselyte and one born into the monotheistic faith. Abraham, therefore, is not simply the proto-type of the convert; he also shows how spiritual fulfillment is possible.

Chapter 4

Paths to the Heights

We may now focus on the ascent of the heaven-born man. A member of this class alone has the free will to determine the shape of his life for good or for evil. In choosing good, he has two paths open to him, that of Abraham and that of Bezalel. Both paths lead ultimately to the same end, the knowledge of God. In either case, the aspirant will require the aid of the encyclia. It is no accident that in characterizing the types of men in *Gig.* 60, Philo called the heaven-born, "votaries of the arts and knowledge" and devotees to the encyclia. In the ensuing chapter, the extent to which this statement is so will be borne out.

1. Encyclical Analogies and Their Interpretations

In his depiction of the encyclia, Philo uses several figures or images which provide analogies to the encyclical studies. The main analogy used by Philo is that which depicts "the culture of the schools" as the "bond-servant (*doulē*) of philosophy" (*Cong.* 79). Drawing on a tradition which allegorized Penelope as philosophy and her handmaids as "ordinary studies,"[1] Philo changes the names, but retains the hierarchical relations of the subjects involved. More specifically, Hagar, the handmaid of Sarah, is seen as the encyclia. Thus Philo writes,

> Sarah, virtue, bears . . . the same relation to Hagar, education, as the mistress to the servant-maid (*therapainida*), or the lawful wife to the concubine . . . (*Cong.* 23).

This analogy, which is the first of many to appear in *De Congressu,* is the dominant image of that treatise.[2]

In addition to appearing as Hagar, in the same treatise the encyclia are also compared with the following: the outer doors of a house and the suburbs of a city (*Cong.* 10), vassals (*Cong.* 18), "simple and milky foods of infancy" (*Cong.* 19), "the earthly and Egyptian body" (*Cong.* 20) and a sojourner (*paroikos, Cong.* 22–23).[3] Turning to Philo's other works, we find elaborations of the analogies noted above:

> Just as gateways are the beginnings of a house, so are the preliminary exercises of the schools (*ta enkyklia propaideumata*) the beginning of virtue (*Fug.* 183).

> Seeing that for babes milk is food, but for grown men wheaten bread, there must also be soul-nourishment, such as is milk-like suited to the time of childhood, in the shape of the preliminary stages of school-learning, and

such as is adapted to grown men in the shape of instructions leading the way through wisdom and temperance and all virtue (*Agr.* 9).[4]

He who contents himself with the secular learning only does but sojourn and is not domiciled with wisdom. He sheds indeed over the soul . . . a sweet fragrance from the exquisite niceties of his studies, but yet it is food, not fragrance, that he needs for his health (*Sac.* 44).

An examination of Philo's corpus reveals other analogies. In *Ebr.* 47–51, the encyclia are symbolized as the younger (lesser) sister, Rachel; Leah is philosophy. At an earlier point in the same treatise, encyclical studies are compared to the mother. Superior to her is the father who is, according to Philo, "reason, masculine, perfect" (*Ebr.* 33).[5] Finally, in *Cher.* 104–5, the encyclia appear in perhaps their most lowly form—as mere "ornaments of the soul. . . . For as stuccoes, paintings, and tablets and arrangements of precious stones . . . contribute nothing to the strength of the building, but only serve to give pleasure to the inmates, so the knowledge of the schools (*hē tōn enkykliōn epistēmē*) adorns the whole house of the soul."

These, then, are some of the more obvious encyclical analogies used by Philo.[6] All of them are characterized by the general inferiority and/or temporal priority of the encyclia relative to some other image whether expressed or implied. With so many similar analogies as evidence, scholars have stressed the subordinate, purely propaedeutic value of encyclical studies. The consensus of scholarly opinion on this subject may be represented by a quotation from Drummond, who wrote in 1888:

So, in every instance, these [encyclical] studies are treated as merely preparatory, of no intrinsic value, but sharpening the mind, and training it for the investigation of more important subjects.[7]

Among the scholars who agree with the interpretation offered above is Leisegang, who claims that "Die Naturwissenschaft hat keinen selbständigen Wert. . . ."[8] In presenting his argument, Leisegang cites *Mut.* 76, a passage which deserves closer attention:

Literally his [Abraham's] name was changed, actually he changed over from nature-study (*physiologias*) to ethical philosophy (*ēthikēn philosophian*) and abandoned the study of the world to find a new home in the knowledge of its Maker, and from this he gained piety (*eusebeian*), the most splendid of possessions.

Mut. 76 reveals the two aspects of the patriarch's experience with the encyclia: first, his devotion to the study of the physical world and then his achievement of the goals of the sage. Abram/Abraham's dual nature reflects the different points of view from which the encyclia may be seen. From Abram's perspective, the encyclia are vital; from that of Abraham, they become unimportant, along with the rest of the mundane world.[9] Only for the man who has successfully ascended to the level of a sage is it correct to say that the encyclia are propaedeutic.[10]

Abraham's example allows us to make one generalization: that is, the "true" value of the discipline is entirely dependent upon the hierarchical position of the learner. Since it is possible to understand the encyclia only in terms of a particular student's progress, the remainder of this chapter will be devoted to a close study of the role of the encyclia in the life of the heaven-born man who rises to become a sage and, then, in the life of the heaven-born man who remains at his station.

2. The Encyclia in the Ascent of the Heaven-born Man to the Life of the Sage

Because of Philo's apparent repugnance for comprehensive accounts,[11] we cannot point to one continuous presentation of the stages of ascent in heaven-born man. In order to construct a systematic account, it will be necessary to draw on several treatises. This procedure may be justified by the fact that the various passages take on a new coherence. A brief summary of the stages may be given here.[12] Beginning with the encyclia, we find that if a student probes the disciplines deeply enough, he precipitates a period of skepticism or, in some formulations, speechlessness. Skepticism, which arises from doubts concerning the external world, leads a man to turn within. Upon introspection, he becomes aware of the nothingness of his own being. This insight in its turn produces a direct apprehension of the greatness of God.[13]

The details of the process described here emerge, in the first instance, when the student of the encyclia realizes that the disciplines only produce conflicting explanations without any solutions. While men may offer conjectures about the world, they can never tell truths about it.[14] These realizations lead a man who wishes to become a sage to a state of skepticism. As pedagogue and philosopher, Philo produces this stage in his readers by drawing on doxographical sources which, taken together, point to the impossibility of certain knowledge:

> Heaven has sent to us no sure indication of its nature, but keeps it beyond our comprehension. For what can we say? That it is a fixed mass of crystal, as some have thought? Or that it is absolutely pure fire? Or that it is a fifth substance, circular in movement, with no part in the four elements? Again, we ask, has the fixed and outmost sphere upward-reaching depth, or is it nothing but a superficies, without depth, resembling plane geometrical figures? Again: are the stars lumps of earth full of fire? Some people have

declared them to be dells and glades and masses of fiery metal. . . . Are they living and intelligent, or devoid of intelligence and conscious life? . . .

Yes, all these and suchlike points pertaining to heaven, that fourth and best cosmic substance, are obscure and beyond our apprehension, based on guess-work and conjecture (*stochasmois kai eikasiais*), not on the solid reasoning of truth; so much so that one may confidently take one's oath that the day will never come when any mortal shall be competent to arrive at a clear solution of any of these problems (*Som.* i.21–24).[15]

What is particularly significant here is that the study of an encyclical discipline *produces* skepticism. In other words, the encyclia themselves provide the motive force for man's movement away from the world of sensation.

A student of the encyclia not only finds himself confronted by conflicting hypotheses about the cosmos. He soon discovers that his senses, which he uses to make judgments concerning the encyclia, are inherently frail. "Each sense impedes [the] attainment of knowledge," Philo remarks in *Jos.* 142, "seduced whether by the sights it sees or by the sounds it hears, or by varieties of flavours, or by scents of different quality. . . . And thus the senses produce the confusion of high with low and great with small, and all that is akin to inequality and irregularity. . . ." In *Praem.* 29, Philo says that reason, the highest expression of human nature, breaks down in the face of sense-objects:

> Reason, sense-perception's master, who thinks itself appointed to judge things conceptual, which ever continue in the same stay, is found to be in sore trouble on many points. For when it comes to grapple with the vast number of particular subjects it becomes incapable, grows exhausted and collapses like an athlete flung prostrate by superior power.

With this we have probably reached the primary reason for Philo's rejection of astronomy, the encyclia in general, and all other conclusions based on sense perception.[16] Sensation itself can never be trusted. This insight leads Philo to a full-scale attack on sense perception in *De Ebrietate,* which begins by associating the frailties of human perception with a skeptical cast of thought:

> If it were always the case that the same objects produced the same impressions on the mind without any variation, it would perhaps be necessary that the two instruments of judgement which nature has established in us, sense and mind, should be held in high esteem as veracious and incorruptible, and that we should not suspend our judgement on any point through doubt but accept a single presentation of two different objects, and on the faith of this choose one and reject the other.
>
> But since we prove to be differently affected by them at different times, we can say nothing with certainty about anything, because the picture presented to us is not constant, but subject to changes manifold and multiform (*Ebr.* 169–70).

Philo's work from this point to *Ebr.* 202 constitutes an important moment in the history of ancient philosophy, for it is the earliest surviving version of the Ten Points against Dogmatism (*tropes*). Of the ten tropes later attributed to Aenesidemus, Philo records eight.[17] The first seven (*Ebr.* 171–92) indicate that brute sense perception cannot be a faithful guide to reality. The senses perceive something akin to a Heracleitean flux in physical reality: differences in the impressions received by various living creatures, individual men, and even one particular man under different conditions, the perspective and the medium through which an object is viewed, etc., all introduce uncertainty of a most elemental sort.[18] Although these tropes are not generated from problems raised by the encyclia in particular, it is obvious that the tropes apply to the encyclical disciplines insofar as they are parts of the material world. Indeed because the encyclia are dependent upon sensation for their very existence and because they require observations which are more precise than those of everyday life, encyclical study would seem to provide the perfect occasion for discovering the truth of the tropes.

The eighth trope which Philo presents, unlike those discussed above, goes beyond mere misperception. Since it has been argued that this trope undermines Philo's own principles, we should consider it in detail:

> And are we not warned against giving over-ready credence to uncertainties by other considerations? . . . By these I mean of course ways of life from boyhood upwards, traditional usages, ancient laws, not a single one of which is regarded in the same light universally, but every country, nation and city, or rather every village and house, indeed every man, woman and infant child takes a totally different view of it. As a proof of this we see that what is base with us is noble with others, what is seemly and just with us is unseemly or unjust with them, our holy is their unholy, our lawful their unlawful, our laudable their blameworthy, our meritorious their criminal, and in all other matters their judgement is the opposite of ours (*Ebr.* 193–94).

> Since then the divers customs of divers persons are not distinguished merely by some slight difference, but exhibit an absolute contrast, amounting to bitter antagonism, it is inevitable that the impressions made upon the mind should differ and that the judgements formed should be at war with each other. In view of these facts, who is so senseless and deranged as to assert positively that any particular thing is just or prudent or honourable or profitable? . . .(*ibid.*, 196–97).

> Now I for my part do not wonder that the chaotic and promiscuous multitude who are bound in inglorious slavery to usages and customs introduced anyhow, and who are indoctrinated from the cradle with the lesson of obedience to them . . . should give vent to affirmations and negations without inquiry or examination. But I do wonder that the multitude of so-

called philosophers, who feign to be seeking for exact and absolute certainty in things, are divided into troops and companies and propound
dogmatic conclusions widely different and often diametrically opposite not
on some single chance point, but on practically all points great or small,
which constitute the problems which they seek to solve (*ibid.,* 198).

Referring primarily to these passages, Colson suggests that Philo "seems to
overthrow the basis of his philosophy." Colson thinks, furthermore, that in
presenting the tropes "Philo seems to jettison his general dogmatic principles
and to enroll himself in the school of the Sceptics."[19]

What Colson fails to realize is that the tropes refer to the material world or
to the act of sensation itself. That is, the issues raised by the tropes would, in
Platonic terms, be assigned to the lower half of the Divided Line. To be sure,
Philo observes that the laws and customs of the nations differ. But this observation reflects only the frailty of *human* law-making.[20] The reader's immediate
reaction is meant to be one of skepticism regarding social conventions which
do not have divine sanction. The primacy of the Torah, however, is
untouched.[21] Essentially Philo's awareness that in everyday life men in different societies are guided by different ordinances is similar to Plato's awareness
that shadows dance on the walls of the Cave. In neither case is the core of the
philosopher's thought affected.

Yet Colson has a point; for instance, Philo treats the issue of providence
skeptically in *Ebr.* 199 while elsewhere he affirms his belief in providence.[22]
This apparent inconsistency is dispelled when we consider that the controversy
generated by the juxtaposition of opinions in *Ebr.* 199 does not take place on a
high spiritual plane, but rather on the level of mere opinion.[23] Philo indicates
as much by attributing conflicting hypotheses to "so-called (*legomenōn*) philosophers, who feign to be seeking for exact and absolute certainty. . ." (*ibid.,*
198). "So-called philosophers" seem to be identical in this respect to
"sophists who propound opinions contrary to each other or even totally and
generically opposed" (*Mut.* 10).[24] As long as minds remain attuned to the
world of the encyclia or sense perception, strife exists, for "truth flees from
the credulous mind which deals in conjecture" (*ton pithanon kai stochastikon
noun, Heres* 248). Real philosophers, on the other hand, do not hold disparate
opinions since, unlike those dealing in conjecture, they are attuned to "dogmatic conclusions"—which is to say the truths of wisdom itself (*Cong.* 142).

Ebr. 199 may be read in this light. There are two distinct modes of thought.
To a sophist, *Ebr.* 199 offers the various possibilities for debate; even to a
student of the encyclia, it reveals issues which seem to elude human capacity.
But to a man who has worked through the encyclia and has acquired the perspective of a philosopher, the material is transformed. On some subjects, with
sophia, he will have acquired the truth. On others, he will at least be better
equipped to undertand the basis of the controversy. Certain issues and

hypotheses might even appear the same; what is different is the eye of the beholder.

The preceding paragraph points to a serious question: how do "outsiders" distinguish intellectually between the false dogmatism of the sophist and the true conclusions of the sage? What makes the difference is that the sage has a "foundation" for his views:

> The sophist is wild in thought, while the wise man is civil. . . . Therefore (Scripture) adds, "his hands against all, and the hands of all against him" [Gen. xvi.12], for, being trained in wide learning and much knowledge, he contradicts all men. (He is) like those who are now called Academics and Sceptics, who place no foundation under their opinions and doctrines and do not (prefer) one thing to another. . . (*QG* iii.33).[25]

The "foundation" of the wise man consists in having transcended both the skeptical phase discussed above and several other phases which we consider below.

In certain contexts a period of speechlessness plays an active role in man's spiritual progress. In many ways, this period seems to be the outer manifestation of skepticism. That is, it either signals the onset of skepticism or is equivalent to it. Several passages on speechlessness stand out. In *Det.* 38, Philo attributes a pregnant silence to Moses:

> [Moses] is not merely not eloquent but absolutely "speechless" (Exod. vi. 12). He calls himself "speechless" (*alogos*), not in the sense in which we use the word of animals without reason, but of him who fails to find a fitting instrument in the language uttered by the organs of speech, and prints and impresses on his understanding the lessons of true wisdom, the direct opposite of false sophistry.

Even more apropos is the fact that Abraham, the prototype of encyclical progress, also has a speechless phase. In the opening sections of *De Migratione,* Philo takes the Lord's injunction to Abraham (Gen. 12.1–3) to mean that he (Abraham) should "quit speech." As Philo writes,

> Quit speech also, "thy father's house," as Moses calls it, for fear thou shouldst be beguiled by beauties of mere phrasing, and be cut off from the real beauty, which lies in the matter expressed. Monstrous it is that shadow should be preferred to substance or a copy to originals. And verbal expression is like a shadow or copy, while the essential bearing of the matters conveyed by words resembles substance and originals (*sōmasi de kai archetypois*); and it behoves the man, whose aim it is to be rather than to seem, to dissociate himself from the former and hold fast to the latter (*Mig.* 12).

Finally there is a more general, less personal statement which Philo attributes to a mind which is "under the divine afflatus." This mind tells a tale which involves a period of speechlessness:

> I [the liberated mind] migrated from the body when I had ceased to regard the flesh; from sense, when I came to view all the objects of sense as having no true existence, when I denounced its standards of judgement as spurious and corrupt and steeped in false opinion . . . from speech, when I sentenced it to long speechlessness (*alogian*), in spite of all its self-exaltation and self-pride. Great indeed was its audacity, that it should attempt the impossible task to use shadows to point me to substances, words to point me to facts. And, amid all its blunders it chattered and gushed about, unable to present with clear expression those distinctions in things which baffled its vague and general vocabulary (*Heres* 71–72).[26]

Elsewhere, instead of alluding specifically to speechlessness, Philo refers to "men of great learning [who] accuse themselves of terrible ignorance . . ." (*Plant.* 80). This also is a consequence of probing a subject too deeply.[27]

Significantly enough, skepticism or speechlessness has a distinct place within the epistemological scheme we have adopted. Wolfson, it will be recalled, divides knowledge of the mind into two types: "rational knowledge, such as a knowledge of the various sciences which ultimately rests on sensation and . . . knowledge of the ideas which does not rest on sensation at all."[28] Since these two kinds of knowledge are utterly different, we cannot picture the aspirant's advance in terms of a gradual continuum. Philo recognizes the discontinuity and makes room for a distinct hiatus in the learning process:

> It is out of the question that those who have sped as far as the edge of wisdom and have just come for the first time into contact with its borders should be conscious of their own perfecting, that both things cannot come about at the same time, the arrival at the goal and the apprehension of the arrival, but that ignorance must form a border-land between the two, not that ignorance which is far removed from knowledge, but that which is close at hand and hard by her door (*Agr.* 161).

Philo speaks here of a period of ignorance prior to wisdom or the knowledge of ideas. The "border-land" to which *Agr.* 161 refers clearly belongs between that knowledge which rests on sensation and that which does not. This is a moment of epistemological crisis, a period of darkness[29] at the end of which man comes to the stage of self-knowledge.

More than once Philo conflates the stages through which a man comes to knowledge.[30] In both of the passages quoted below Philo moves directly from mistrust of the encyclical world to a call for self-knowledge:

> Come forward now, you who are laden with vanity and gross stupidity and vast pretence, you that are wise in your own conceit and not only declare

(in every case) that you perfectly know what each object is, but go so far as
to venture in your audacity to add the reasons for its being what it is, as
though you had either been standing by at the creation of the world, and
had observed how and out of what materials its several parts were
fashioned, or had acted as advisers to the Creator regarding the things He
was forming. . . (*Mig.* 136)

For pray do not, O ye senseless ones, spin your airy fables about moon
or sun or the other objects in the sky and in the universe so far removed
from us and so varied in their natures, until you have scrutinized and come
to know yourselves. After that, we may perhaps believe you when you hold
forth on other subjects: but before you establish who you yourselves are,
do not think that you will ever become capable of acting as judges or trust-
worthy witnesses in other matters (*ibid.*, 138).

The same observation could be made based on another passage, *Mig.* 184–85;

How strange it is, my friends, that you have been suddenly lifted to such a
height above the earth and are floating there, and, leaving the lower air
beneath you, are treading the ether above, thinking to master every detail
respecting the movements of the sun, and of the circuits of the moon, and
of the glorious rhythmical dances of the other constellations. These are too
high to be reached by your powers of thought. . . . Come down therefore
from heaven, and, when you have come down, do not begin in turn to pass
in review earth and sea and rivers, and plants and animals in their various
kinds; but explore yourselves only and your own nature. . . .

The movement toward self-knowledge in Philo is depicted here as the result
of Abraham's experience with astronomy.[31] But given Philo's analysis of sense
perception and the fact that the encyclia are part of that world, he could have
come to the same conclusion from an analysis of other disciplines. For basically they are all cut from the same cloth, and the realizations of the student
are the same regardless of which particular discipline gave rise to them.

Once the world of sensation fails, there is no alternative but to obey the
Delphic Oracle and look inward.[32] This process creates a sense of personal
nothingness, as we see in *Spec.* i.264:

He [Moses] holds that the most profitable form of purification is just this,
that a man should know himself and the nature of the elements of which he
is composed, ashes and water, so little worthy of esteem.

Despair, based on one's sense of nothingness, brings about the ultimate
knowledge of God, man's final goal:

When most he [Abraham] knew himself, then most did he despair of himself, in order that he might attain to an exact knowledge of Him Who in

reality IS. And this is nature's law: he who has thoroughly comprehended himself, thoroughly despairs of himself, having as a step to this ascertained the nothingness in all respects of created being. And the man who has despaired of himself is beginning to know Him that IS (*Som.* i.60).[33]

This final stage is also depicted in *Mig.* 195. In that passage, Philo says:

When, having opened up the road that leads from self, in hope thereby to come to discern the Universal Father, so hard to trace and unriddle, it will crown maybe the accurate self-knowledge it has gained with the knowledge of God Himself.

These, then, are the stages of spiritual ascent for the sage: skepticism (or speechlessness) growing out of the encyclia, realization of the nothingness of created being, self-knowledge, self-despair (a sense of personal nothingness growing out of introspection), and finally knowledge of God. Several other remarks should be made concerning the ascent. Often Philo skips a stage in his account or he connects two phases in order to emphasize the dynamics of spiritual progress. For instance, having a sense of one's personal nothingness leads directly to the opposite—a realization of God's All and of our dependence on him.[34] From dramatic juxtapositions such as these we may infer that man ascends by negations, by grasping opposites.

After a long struggle, the sage finally gains wisdom or knowledge of God. He also acquires faith, as Philo explicitly says in his treatise on reward and punishment. In that work Philo first describes the career of Abraham, the paradigm of a heaven-born man who ascends to the level of the sage. Then Philo continues,

The leader [Abraham] in adopting the godly creed, who first passed over from vanity to truth, came to his consummation by virtue gained through instruction, and he received for his reward belief in God (*tēn pros theon pistin, Praem.* 27).

And so some men reach the highest goal, proceeding like Abraham by the direct method. What is significant is that the movement toward the goals of the sage begins with skepticism regarding the encyclical world. This is not a phase which can be passed over lightly, for his ascent hangs in the balance. Without prior "knowledge" of and skepticism concerning the encyclia no man can emulate Abraham. At the early stages of one's progress, all things are obscure. But arriving at the journey's end, the sage will reflect on his ascent and realize the critical nature of the encyclical stages of his sojourn.

3. The Encyclia in the Ascent of the Heaven-born Man Who Remains at His Station

The indirect path to knowledge of God, the path which proceeds "from down to up," is that taken by Bezalel.[35] Although he is the prototypical traveller along this route, most of our discussion will be based on the class of ordinary men as a whole. The following passage should recall these men to mind:

> Those who are unable by virtue to beget fine and praiseworthy deeds ought to pursue intermediate education, and in a certain sense produce children from the school studies, for wide learning is a sort of whetstone of the mind and reason. . . . While it is imperfect it is sufficient for it to have a milder and gentler teaching which comes through the school studies. Whence it is not for nothing that in the sacred athletic contests those who cannot take the first prizes in the contest are deserving of the second (*QG* iii.20).

We shall consider the progressive man here in his relationship to the encyclia. Since Philo believed that each man should be seen in terms of his métier,[36] such a conjunction is a natural one. What is more, it will allow us to see certain functions of the arts and sciences which hitherto have been overlooked.[37]

We shall begin with the very substance of the ordinary man's intellectual world—the conjectures which he formulates about the material world.[38] Owing to the infinity of the disciplines and their ultimate unknowability, the man of progress is limited to conjectures.[39] He can move with these, however, from the part to the whole, as Philo indicates in *Som.* i.204:

> Though I am incapable of seeing even the smallest part of it, but from the part brought within the range of my vision . . . I form in detail a conjecture about the whole on the strength of what analogy leads me to expect.

That Philo is referring to the activity of the student of the encyclia here is made explicit in *Som.* i.205, where he stresses the student's ability to take what is essential from each discipline:

> From these combined he frames a single work gay and bright to a degree, blending wide learning with readiness to learn still more.

As if these allusions were not sufficient to identify the student, Philo continues,

> The artificer of this fabric was called by the holy word (*ho hieros logos*) Bezalel (Ex. xxxi.2ff.), which is when interpreted "in the shadow of God." For it is the copies of which he is chief builder, whereas Moses builds the patterns . . . (*Som.* i.206).[40]

Returning to *Som.* i.204, we may take note of how the student moves by analogy from the part to the whole. This process is repeated elsewhere on a grander scale when the student moves from partial "knowledge" of the disciplines to knowledge of God. Formally speaking, this movement "from down to up" is a teleological argument for the existence of God from the design of the universe:[41]

> Anyone entering this world, as it were some vast house or city, and behold-

ing the sky circling round and embracing within it all things, and planets
and fixed stars without any variation moving in rhythmical harmony and
with advantage to the whole, and earth with the central space assigned to it,
water and air flowing in set order as its boundary . . . will surely argue that
these have not been wrought without consummate art, but that the Maker
of this whole universe was and is God (*LA* iii.99).[42]

The same point is made in *Special Laws*; here, as in the previous quotation, the
student of the encyclia is the obvious protagonist:

None of the works of human art is self-made, and the highest art and
knowledge is shewn in this universe, so that surely it has been wrought by
one of excellent knowledge and absolute perfection. In this way we have
gained the conception of the existence of God (*Spec.* i.35).

Since we have identified these arguments in Philo, it would be well to assess
their status as propositions. Philo gives some indication of his view by
remarking that those "who are at pains to discern the Uncreated, and Creator
of all from His creation" are making a "happy guess" (*stochastai, Praem.* 46).
This passage seems to indicate that teleological arguments do not have the
authority or truth-value of direct knowledge; yet inferring the universe from
creation still is the highest form of inference that an ordinary man can make.
In several passages, teleological arguments grow out of the study of astronomy, "the queen of the sciences." From Philo's point of view, such a lofty
origin would tend to enhance the value of the argument itself. But it should
not be thought that divine insight develops exclusively from astronomical
observations. For any discipline which *orders* phenomena in the physical universe may lead to knowledge of God from design.[43] The only requirement is
that one should gain an appreciation for the design of the cosmos from the
order of the art or science.[44] Certainly this is the point of view expressed in
Fug. 213:

How couldst thou fail, thou soul, who in thy progress art dipping deep into
the school-lore knowledge (*tē tōn enkykliōn epistēmē propaideumatōn*), to see
reflected in thy training as in a mirror the Author of that knowledge?

In concluding, we should consider the following quotation:

Service pleasing to God and to virtue is like an intense and severe harmony,
and in no soul is there an instrument capable of sustaining it, without such
frequent relaxation and unstringing of the chords that it descends from the
higher forms of art to the lower (*epi tas mesas . . . technas, Sac.* 37–38).

This passage seems to refer to all men who strive to attain the heights. Regardless of their points of departure, men return to the lower forms of art, or the
encyclia. The passage may be applied to the ordinary, progressive man on

whom the movement "from down to up" is undoubtedly a strain. But it also seems to apply to a man like Abraham who needs to recover from the intensity of having achieved his goal.[45]

Apart from the refreshment which the encyclia provide, what can they offer men who have attained as much as their individual natures allow? Because the disciplines are infinite, they are a source for perpetual reflection on the wonders of the universe. Philo seems to have believed that searching the universe, despite the impossibility of coming to a full and final understanding, is a value in itself.[46] The encyclical disciplines then are perfect objects for such a search. But more important, the encyclia are a mirror to which both sage and ordinary men always return to see a reflection of the divine presence.

A certain Philosopher asked St. Anthony: Father, how can you be so happy when you are deprived of the consolation of books? Anthony replied: My book, O philosopher, is the nature of created things, and any time I want to read the words of God, the book is before me.[47]

Conclusion

Philo's treatment of the encyclical studies exemplifies the mixture of appropriation and rejection which is typical of his response to Greek culture in general. We can put this generalization into sharper focus by considering Philo's reaction to Plato's system of education as it is set forth in the *Republic*. From a philosophical point of view, Philo appropriates the elitism of Platonic educational theory with little modification. For Philo's sage, as for Plato's guardian, the arts and sciences are merely the first propaedeutic step toward understanding the truth.[1] Hence there are striking similarities between Philo's Moses and Plato's philosopher-king, not the least of which is the curriculum which they followed.[2] In the careers of both, encyclical studies occupy a subordinate position compared with the final goal of *sophia*.

When Philo introduces a theological perspective, however, he departs from Plato's elitism. It is true that Philo's sage is a spiritual as well as a philosophical aristocrat. But Philo is also concerned with the religious progress of ordinary men who venture forth on "second-best" voyages. For men like Bezalel, knowledge of the encyclia is not simply the first propaedeutic step toward the attainment of true knowledge. Rather, mastery of the encyclia is for them a major theological accomplishment. Only through a study of creation can they arrive at knowledge of God. Here Philo is clearly adapting Greek material to his own needs. By placing the arts and sciences within a distinctly Jewish theological context, Philo modifies and transforms the traditional content of encyclical education.

If Philo had appropriated only the more abstract doctrines of Greek philosophy his borrowings would have been interesting, but not otherwise remarkable. After all, the higher reaches of Greek thought have proven inviting to philosophers of different religious persuasions throughout the ages. One need only cite the early Christian attachment to Plato or Maimonides' creative adaptation of Aristotle in order to establish the affinity of monotheistic theologians to Greek philosophy. But Philo deliberately chose the encyclia, the most mundane strata of the Greek heritage, and his incorporation of those everyday disciplines points to a strong desire on Philo's part to accommodate himself to his cultural environment.

The challenge of Greek thought and Philo's response to that challenge is by no means unparalleled in the history of culture. McKeon, writing about the phenomenon in a general way, has observed:

> In all three monotheistic religions, those who feared the pagan arts and learning as distractions from the good life or as sources of error were opposed to those who sought to use human knowledge to supplement and support human formulations of divine wisdom.[3]

Philo neither feared pagan learning nor felt ill at ease with it.[4] Taking it for granted that the elite Jewish youth of Alexandria would be enrolled in Greek institutions,[5] he appears to have asked himself in what way their secular education could be turned to account. Jews, he insisted, should utilize the encyclia in their strivings toward divine knowledge instead of exploiting the acquisition of Greek culture simply to further their social and political ambitions.[6] If Jewish youth were driven (for whatever reason) to acquire the culture of the day, they could do so within a Jewish context. Philo sought to provide that context for knowledge which originated in secular institutions.

In this environment, the social and political lures of total assimilation must have loomed large. Philo was particularly sensitive to this issue, perhaps because his nephew, Tiberius Julius Alexander, had already shown signs of disloyalty to Judaism. Yet despite the dangers, Philo himself was irresistibly drawn by the obvious attractions of the Greek legacy. This does not mean that Philo was lax in his affiliation to the Jewish faith. Philo continued to draw clear lines between what was acceptable and what was not acceptable for his coreligionists. To him it was advisable for Jews with inquiring minds to allegorize Scripture; it was a mistake for them to follow the extreme allegorists into nonobservance. Likewise, a Jew could participate in pagan entertainments during weekdays, but the Sabbath was still to be set aside for the study of Torah.[7] In the same spirit, Philo encourages a certain devotion to the encyclia, but he places them within a Jewish framework, and he repeatedly warns against their seductive charms.[8] On the latter point, I cannot emphasize too strongly the real dangers which Philo saw in the disciplines, dangers which ranged from sophistry to heresy. Yet the benefits which the encyclia offered to ordinary man and sage alike were of such value that Philo could not proscribe the secular disciplines.

One does not have to go far afield—either geographically or chronologically—to find opposition to Philo from a traditional point of view; it existed at home among the Alexandrian Jewish literalists.[9] But there are many indications that Philo advocated a form of Judaism which was especially adapted to meet the spiritual and intellectual needs of a specific circle of Alexandrian Jews. Perhaps the independence of mind of this community goes back to the translation of the Pentateuch.[10] Philo, in recounting the events leading up to this translation, is careful to stress that the Seventy "had received an education in Greek as well as in their native lore" (*Mos.* ii.32). So Philo himself was aware that the particular fusion of Greek and Jewish culture, of which he was the most eloquent spokesman, had a long history.

Jews of Philo's persuasion would have upheld and observed what they perceived to be the basic tenets of the faith. But then, where traditional beliefs or practices conflicted with contemporary perceptions of reality, they would have turned to Alexandrian Jewish exegetes, who must have been reconciling their spiritual dilemmas for generations. Philo, perhaps the last and greatest of these exegetes, had various tools at his disposal. With allegory, he could shed new light on old truths; with Greek philosophy, he could offer new reasons for old practices. Resorting to these devices, Philo could retain Scripture while he accommodated himself and his followers to the intellectual challenge of the age.

In an earlier chapter, I mentioned the need of Philo's circle to arrive at a balance between traditional forms of Judaism and the exigencies of life in Alexandria. How should we conceive of Philo's role in such a situation? Undoubtedly, Philo was involved in offering acceptable rationalizations for those elements of the tradition which he thought it essential to retain (e.g., circumcision in *Spec.* i.1–7).[11] At the same time there were specifically local elements (e.g., the Greek translation of Scripture as related in *Mos.* ii.25–44) and issues on which Alexandrian custom had established itself as normative. On the latter front, Philo seems to have served as transmitter of Alexandrian Jewish philosophy. Finally, he made an original contribution of his own which he often enriched by drawing on such elements from the classical world as suited his purpose.

Present-day students who are unsympathetic to Philo's diverse roles conjure up an image of an Alexandrian picking and choosing almost at random from the religious baggage of the Hellenistic world. The term "eclectic" has often been used to epitomize this activity. I would argue, however, that Philo's appropriation of "foreign" elements was deliberate. Appropriation, for him, necessitated the drawing of lines. If Philo drew from different sources, he also constructed a fence around his conception of Judaism. Working and living in an area where the boundary between "Greek" and "Jewish" was blurred and having integrated pagan learning into the heart of his religious philosophy, Philo had to indicate where the appropriation could begin and where it had to end.

By endowing the encyclia with positive value, Philo sought to reconcile several oppositions. He hoped to make human disciplines compatible with the divine; on this theoretical level, Philo was successful. But he also seems to have offered the encyclia as a common ground between the Greek and the Jewish worlds. There is an element of pathos in his attempt, for it was the last such effort. On both sides fanatical hatred was building up. As Tcherikover observed, the fall of Jerusalem sealed the fate not only of the Jews of Palestine, but of Egypt as well.[12]

With the failure of true reconciliation between Greek and Jew, all hopes for a viable form of Judaism based on Philonic principles faded. The route which Philo advocated thus ended in a cul-de-sac. Only a historian, with the vision of a backward-looking prophet, can suggest reasons for the failure of Philo's endeavor. First of all, Philo's writings were sufficiently abstract that they could not have had wide currency. Although we have heard Philo speaking of the ordinary man in this monograph, he was referring to spiritual categories. His concept of the encyclia itself was not a revolutionary one aimed at bringing knowledge of God to all social classes. Like the rest of his philosophy, it was directed exclusively to an educated aristocratic audience. Secondly, Greek and Jewish reconciliation may not have been a real alternative at any point during Philo's lifetime. The Greeks had long-standing grievances with the Jews, grievances which might have been too deep for Philo's philosophical circle to overcome. The pogrom of the year 38 was only one sign of the rift between the communities. Thirdly, the events of 66–70 C.E. might have sapped the strength of the most vigorous fringe movement within Judaism. To put it another way, the effort to preserve what was to become mainstream Judaism may have taken place at the expense of more individual voices, such as Philo's.

If these considerations do not explain the failure of Philo's effort, his adoption by the Church was sufficient to assure him of oblivion within Judaism for centuries to come. In this regard, Philo's tendency to look beyond the literal text of Scripture may have been altogether too successful in non-Jewish circles for it to have retained an honored place within Judaism as it was then emerging. But we should not judge Philo by the fact that the paths he charted did not prove viable within "mainstream" Judaism. The political upheavals and religious challenges which were awaiting Judaism in the second half of the first century were unprecedented in Jewish history. In turning to the Greek world and in accepting parts of what it had to offer, Philo sought to preserve that form of Judaism which to him seemed most vital. He did so out of a deep conviction that Jewish scripture, mediated by the wisdom of Greece, would provide an answer to the cultural crisis of his time.

Notes

INTRODUCTION

1. See Menahem Stern, *Greek and Latin Authors on Jews and Judaism: From Herodotus to Plutarch* (Jerusalem, 1976), pp. 47–52, for classical references and relevant bibliography.

2. Trans. H. St. J. Thackeray in *LCL* (London, 1926).

3. Victor A. Tcherikover, *Hellenistic Civilization and the Jews,* trans. S. Applebaum (Philadelphia, 1959), pp. 40–41.

4. *CPJ,* I, 27–30.

5. Erwin R. Goodenough, *Jewish Symbols in the Greco-Roman Period* (13 vols.; New York, 1953–68), XII, 50ff. Goodenough, *ibid.,* p. 51, refers to one archaeological report from Beth She'arim in which 33 of the 41 inscriptions studied were in Greek.

6. Saul Lieberman, *Hellenism in Jewish Palestine* (2nd ed.; New York, 1962) and *Greek in Jewish Palestine* (New York, 1965).

7. Tcherikover, *Hellenistic Civilization,* p. 41.

8. Only two epigrams from Beth She'arim suggest that their authors were familiar with the Homeric epic: cf. M. Schwabe and B. Lifshitz, *Beth She'arim: The Greek Inscriptions* (New Brunswick, New Jersey, 1974), II, 220.

9. Lieberman, *Hellenism in Jewish Palestine,* p. 3.

10. Harry A. Wolfson, *Philo: Foundations of Religious Philosophy in Judaism, Christianity, and Islam* (2 vols.; 4th printing rev.; Cambridge, 1968), I, 91–92, nn. 32–33.

11. For instance, *Immut.* 35–46 (= *SVF* II, 458b) gives expression to an important aspect of Stoic physics.

12. See my article, "A Reappraisal of Wolfson's Method," *Studia Philonica* 3 (1974–75), 11–26.

13. One could read Philo from beginning to end without getting a sense that every Jewish male actually made a pilgrimage to Jerusalem three times a year. Most scholars now agree that Philo himself did not make regular pilgrimages.

14. Circumcision is an instance of this; cf. the opening paragraphs of Philo's main treatise on law, *Spec.* i.1–11.

15. Cf. *PLCL* IX, 521–22; the editor here correctly points out that Diotima's speech comes close to some of Philo's own thought. Also see Herman L. Sinaiko, *Love, Knowledge, and Discourse in Plato* (Chicago, 1965), pp. 292–93, n. 2, and Meyer W. Isenberg, "The Order of the Discourses in Plato's *Symposium*" (unpublished diss., University of Chicago, 1940).

16. Cf. Wolfson, *Philo,* I, 82–86. I suggest that the reader cull from this statement the basic distinctions within the Alexandrian Jewish community. The doctrinal unity of the Jewish community, as Wolfson conceives of it, is open to question.

17. E. R. Goodenough, "Literal Mystery in Hellenistic Judaism," in *Quantulacumque,* eds. R. P. Casey, S. Lake and A. K. Lake (London, 1937), 227.

18. Wolfson, *Philo,* I, 86.

19. In using rabbinic material we meet two problems: the first is that of terminology and content, and the second, that of dating. The exact content of *ḥokhmah yewanit* is not known with any precision. Nevertheless Lieberman in *Hellenism in Jewish Palestine,* p. 105, has offered a general definition. According to him, *ḥokhmah yewanit* refers to a body of "information which could help the individual in his association with the educated Hellenistic circles of Palestine." Since *ḥokhmah yewanit* is an inexact term, we must use it with caution. In particular we must not assume that there is necessarily any overlap of content between Greek Wisdom and the encyclia.

The second problem in using this concept is that of dating. Because of the paucity of available evidence, we are forced to cite rabbis who lived in different periods. As Shaye Cohen pointed out in an unpublished article, "The Hellenization of Rabbinic Judaism: The State of the Question and Some Suggestions for Further Research" (written for the Consultation on Hellenistic Judaism, Society of Biblical Literature, 1977), p. 14, there is no comprehensive collection of rabbinic statements dealing with our question.

The vagueness of both content and dating preclude any direct use of this material. It is instructive, however, to witness the rabbis' general attitudes to this alien body of information.

20. Until recently the consensus of scholarly opinion was that the rabbis of the Talmud imposed a ban on Greek Wisdom. Lieberman has opposed this contention in *Hellenism in Jewish Palestine*, pp. 100–14 and 210–11. Other voices in this controversy include: G. Alon, *Meḥqarim Be-Toldot Yisra'el* I (Studies in Jewish History), (Tel Aviv, 1967); M. Hengel, *Judaism and Hellenism: Studies in Their Encounter in Palestine during the Early Hellenistic Period* (trans. J. Bowden; 2 vols.; London, 1974), I, 172–73 and n. 440; L. Feldman, "Hengel's *Judaism and Hellenism* in Retrospect," *JBL* 96 (1977), 376–77; Feldman, "Hellenism and the Jews," *Encyclopedia Judaica* (Jerusalem, 1971) 8, 295–301; E. Ebner, *Elementary Education in Ancient Israel during the Tanaitic Period (10–220 C.E.)* (New York, 1956), pp. 84–87; G. Mussies, "Greek in Palestine and the Diaspora," *The Jewish People in the First Century*, ed. S. Safrai and M. Stern (Philadelphia, 1976), II, 1054.

The sources listed above deal specifically with the question of Greek Wisdom and its acceptance or rejection by rabbinic Judaism. This question is but one aspect of a larger study—the relation between Greco-Roman civilization and Judaism, both in Palestine and the Diaspora. H. A. Fischel has made a significant contribution to the latter study in *Essays in Greco-Roman and Related Talmudic Literature* (New York, 1977) by collecting in one volume the articles which have shaped our understanding of the interdependence of Greco-Roman and Jewish thought. Particularly noteworthy in the volume is Fischel's "Prolegomenon" containing an introductory section (pp. XIII–XXIX) and an invaluable annotated chronological bibliography (pp. XXXIV–LXXII).

21. Lieberman, *Hellenism in Jewish Palestine*, p. 104, and *Greek in Jewish Palestine*, pp. 1 and 20.

22. *Idem, Hellenism in Jewish Palestine*, p. 101.

23. S. Safrai, "Education and the Study of the Torah," in *The Jewish People in the First Century*, II, 959. Also see Lieberman, "How Much Greek in Jewish Palestine?" in *Texts and Studies* (New York, 1974), pp. 224–25, and A. Wasserstein, "Astronomy and Geometry as Propaedeutic Studies in Rabbinic Literature" (Hebrew), *Tarbiz* 43 (1973–74), 53–57.

24. Cf. Ebner, *Elementary Education in Ancient Israel*, p. 87.

25. *The Babylonian Talmud, Seder Nashim, Sotah*, trans. A. Cohen (London, 1936). Also see Hengel, *Judaism and Hellenism*, II, 53, n. 153.

26. Feldman, "Hengel's *Judaism and Hellenism*," 380.

27. *The Babylonian Talmud, Seder Kodashim, Menaḥoth*, trans. Eli Cashdan (London, 1948).

28. E. E. Hallewy, "Concerning the Ban on Greek Wisdom" (Hebrew), *Tarbiz* 41 (1972), 269–74. Cohen in "The Hellenization of Rabbinic Judaism . . .," p. 14, agrees (with certain qualifications) that Hallewy's solution to this problem is preferable to Lieberman's.

29. Hallewy, "Concerning the Ban . . .," 272.

30. *Ibid.*, 273.

31. This is Lieberman's explanation in *Hellenism in Jewish Palestine*, pp. 100–102.

32. Hallewy, "Concerning the Ban . . .," 272–73.

33. Cf. Josephus, *Against Apion* I, 179–80.

34. A. Henrichs, "Philosophy, the Handmaiden of Theology," *Greek, Roman, and Byzantine Studies* 9 (1968), 446, provides an interesting parallel. Origen in a letter to Gregory Thaumaturgus wrote: "I should like you to select even from Greek philosophy those encyclopedic disciplines or preliminary studies that can be applied to the Christian teaching, and also those parts of geometry and astronomy that are useful for the exegesis of the Holy Scriptures." (Henrichs' note: Orig. *Ep. ad Greg. Thaum.* 1 [*Philocalia* p. 64, 21ff. Robinson].)

35. Cf. B. Z. Wacholder, *Eupolemus: A Study of Judaeo-Greek Literature* (Monographs of the Hebrew Union College, 3; Cincinnati, 1974), esp. Ch. XI.

36. The translation is that of K. Freeman, *Ancilla to the Pre-Socratic Philosophers* (Cambridge, 1957), p. 139. Although I shall discuss this maxim at greater length in Ch. IV, *infra*, it is worth noting here a brief account of the origin of the maxim in Henrichs, "Philosophy, the Handmaiden of Theology," 444.

37. We can discern in classical and Hellenistic writers a wide diversity of opinions toward the encyclia. There were (1) authors who saw no value in the encyclia at all, (2) authors who emphasized solely the utilitarian value of the disciplines, and finally (3) authors who found in the encyclia a legitimate propaedeutic role. (Cf. M. L. Clarke, *Higher Education in the Ancient World* [London, 1971], pp. 3–5.)

Xenophon (*Memorabilia* iv.7.2–4, 8) emphasized the utilitarian value of geometry, astronomy, and arithmetic—the study of which facilitates one's conduct of practical affairs. Isocrates (*Antidosis* 264–66) regarded the disciplines as "gymnastic of the mind." But both Epicurus and Zeno the Stoic, founders of influential schools of philosophy, took a dim view of *paideia* and *enkyklios paideia*. According to Diogenes Laertius, Epicurus wrote the following letter to one of his students: "Hoist all sail, my dear boy, and steer clear of all culture" (*paideia*, x.6, trans. R. D. Hicks, *LCL*, [London, 1965]). (Perhaps we should take this remark with a grain of salt; cf. A. A. Long, *Hellenistic Philosophy: Stoics, Epicureans, Sceptics* [London, 1974], p. 30). In a similar vein, Zeno of Citium is said to have declared the encyclia "useless" (Diog. L. vii.32).

On a more positive note, Diogenes Laertius attributed the following view to Xenocrates, the third head of the Academy: "To some who had never learnt either music or geometry or astronomy, but nevertheless wished to attend his lectures, Xenocrates said, 'Go your ways, for you offer philosophy nothing to lay hold of'" (iv.10). As a student, Justin Martyr had a similar experience. Justin came to a Pythagorean "who asked if he was acquainted with music, astronomy, and geometry"; see R. M. Grant, *Augustus to Constantine* (London, 1971), p. 133. Also see H. A. Fischel, *Rabbinic Literature and Greco-Roman Philosophy* (Leiden, 1973), p. 15, esp. n. 134, and p. 20.

If, in the time of Zeno the Stoic, the disciplines were rejected because they could not bestow the Stoic *summum bonum* of virtue, three centuries later Seneca was willing to concede that the *liberales artes*, a term which he took to refer to the encyclical studies (*Epistle* 88.23), should have a subordinate role in preparing the soul for the reception of virtue (cf. *ibid.* 88.20). For the Roman career of the *liberales artes*, see J. T. Townsend, "Ancient Education in the Time of the Early Roman Empire" in *The Catacombs and the Colosseum: The Roman Empire as the Setting of Primitive Christianity*, ed. S. Benko and J. J. O'Rourke (Valley Forge, 1971), pp. 139–63. Townsend argues for the continuity of educational theory and practice in the Hellenistic and Roman worlds. Also see H. Chadwick, "Philo and the Beginnings of Christian Thought," *The Cambridge History of Later Greek and Early Medieval Philosophy*, ed. A. H. Armstrong (Cambridge, 1967), p. 140.

38. Learning the disciplines was regarded as essential for the properly cultivated man as is clear from Plato's remark that ignorance of them is "more worthy of a stupid beast like the hog than of a human being." When faced with the comparatively high level of Egyptian learning in arithmetic, the protagonist in the *Laws* says, "I blushed not for myself alone, but for our whole Hellenic world" (*Laws* 819c–d, trans. A. E. Taylor). For a general treatment of this subject, see R. C. Lodge, *Plato's Theory of Education* (London, 1947), especially Ch. II. The translation of the *Republic* cited here is that of P. Shorey, *LCL* (2 vols.; London, 1930).

39. On the history of *enkyklios paideia*, see Marrou, *Saint Augustin et la fin de la culture antique* (Paris, 1938), pp. 211–35 with corrections in his *History*, p. 527, n. 2. Also see H. Koller, "Enkyklios Paideia," *Glotta* 34 (1955), 174–89; F. Kühnert, *Allgemeinbildung und Fachbildung in der Antike* (Deutsche Akademie der Wissenschaften; Berlin, 1961), 30, 7ff.; L. M. de Rijk, "Enkyklios Paideia: A Study of Its Original Meaning," *Vivarium* 3 (1965), 79–85; H. Fuchs, "Enkyklios Paideia," *Reallexikon für Antike und Christentum*, ed. T. Klauser (Stuttgart, 1962), 5, 366–98.

40. F. H. Colson, "Philo on Education," *JTS* 18 (1916–17), 151–62.
41. R. Marcus, "An Outline of Philo's System of Education" (Hebrew), *Sepher Touroff*, ed. I Silberschlag and J. Twersky (Boston, 1938), pp. 223–31.
42. M. Alexandre, *De congressu eruditionis gratia* (trans. and ed.) = vol. 16 of "Les oeuvres de Philon d'Alexandrie," series ed. R. Arnaldez *et al.* (Paris, 1967) and Alexandre, "La culture profane chez Philon," *PAL*, pp. 105–30. I am particularly indebted to Alexandre for raising many relevant issues.
43. Cf. Colson, "Philo's Quotations from the Old Testament," *JTS* 41 (1940), 250.

CHAPTER 1

1. *Paideia* in the second sense has been defined by H. I. Marrou, *A History of Education in Antiquity*, trans. G. Lamb for the New American Library (New York, 1964), p. 142, as "'culture'— not in the sense of something active and preparational like education, but in the sense . . . of something perfected: a mind fully developed, the mind of a man who has become truly man." Also see W. Jentsch, *Urchristliches Erziehungsdenken: Die Paideia Kyriu im Rahmen der hellenistisch-jüdischen Unwelt* (Gütersloh, 1951).
2. See Werner Jaeger, *Paideia: The Ideals of Greek Culture,* trans. G. Highet (3 vols.; Oxford, 1939–45).
3. In recent years two invaluable aids to terminological discussions have appeared: Professor Peder Borgen and Roald Skarsten's key-word-in-context Concordance to Philo (see my preface) and G. Mayer, *Index Philoneus* (Berlin, 1974). I have relied heavily on both these sources.
    The reader will observe various nuances of the word (e.g., "instruction," "training," "discipline") by comparing the following: *LA* ii.90ff., *Sac.* 63, *Post.* 97; *Ebr.* 81, *Plant.* 127, 162, *Heres* 125; *Immut.* 54; *Spec.* ii.21, 229.
4. Jentsch, *Urchristliches Erziehungsdenken . . .*, pp. 119–20, makes specific reference to Philo, especially to *Decal.* 106ff. and *Spec.* ii.224ff.
5. Cf., for instance, *Mut.* 228–29 and *Ebr.* 34.
6. In the year 1531, Sir Thomas Elyot published a book entitled *The Governour* in which the word "encyclopedia" appeared for the first time in English. Introducing "encyclopedia" to his readers, Elyot wrote that the term meant "a heape of all maner of lernynge, which of some is called the worlde of science, of other the circle of doctrine" (London, 1531; folio 48*v*).
7. Marrou, *History*, p. 244.
8. *Ibid.*
9. Alexandre, *De Congressu . . .* (ed.), pp. 31–33.
10. De Rijk, *"Enkyklios Paideia . . .," passim.*
11. Hence *enkyklios paideia* = *choreia paideusis.* De Rijk argues that both of these terms refer to choric education: rhythm, melody, and word (*ibid.*, p. 83; cf. p. 93).
12. *Ibid.*, pp. 40–41.
13. *Ibid.*, pp. 77–78. Here de Rijk draws our attention to the following passages in which Philo links *enkyklios* with "choric terminology": with *choros* and related words, *Mut.* 263 and 229, *Ebr.* 33, *Cher. 3, Cong.* 20, *Post.* 137; with *achoreutos* in an oxymoron, *Leg.* 168; with *arrythmos* and *ametros, Fug.* 42, *Cher.* 105. Also see *Spec.* i. 342–43.
14. A partial list of the synonyms (excluding those discussed above) includes: *enkyklia, propaideumata, enkyklios mousikē, enkyklia mathēmata,* and various synonymous expressions such as those in *Agr.* 9, *Ebr.* 33, and *Cher.* 104.
15. E.g., see *Cong.* 127–28. On Philo's use of *mesē paideia,* see Henrichs, "Philosophy, the Handmaiden . . .," pp. 443–44.
16. *PLCL* I, xvii, note *a.*
17. Philo uses *mesos* in positive senses, for instance, in *Spec.* iv.168, *Mig.* 146, *Immut.* 162–65,

Opif. 154, *Som.* i.68. These examples may be compared to Philo's use of *mesos* in a more neutral sense in *LA* i.93, ii.64, iii.67.

18. Marrou, *Saint Augustin,* p. 219; cf. de Rijk, *"Enkyklios Paideia . . .,"* p. 67. Alexandre, *De Congressu . . .* (ed.), p. 29, n. 3, mentions expressions containing *technē,* but does not discuss them.

19. *Banausoi technai* are also mentioned in *LA* ii.107.

20. This ambiguity has led modern commentators into uncertainty regarding the exact referent of the word. Cf. Colson's difficulties in *Det.* 145 as expressed in his note *PLCL* II, 496. Also see J. Dillon, *The Middle Platonists: A Study of Platonism 80 B.C. to A.D. 220* (London, 1977), p. 145.

21. By picking a time by which the encyclia were well established I do not intend to maintain that they were not previously recognized. Marrou, *History,* p. 528, n. 5, dates "the first appearance of the liberal arts 'septenary' between Dionysius Thrax and Varro" in the first century B.C.E. In following Marrou here it appears necessary to reject T. Davidson, "The Seven Liberal Arts," *Educational Review,* 2 (1891), 470: "At the Christian era no definite number had been fixed for the liberal arts either at Athens, Alexandria, or Rome." Davidson's calculations are by no means aided by the fact that he ignores *Cong.* 11 and concludes that "astronomy appears in none of [Philo's] lists" (*ibid.*). Yet it seems strange that, if Philo was aware of the encyclical studies as a group of seven, he made no attempt to allegorize them as such. According to Davidson, the allegorizing was left for Cassidorus: "Attention was first called to the *number* of the arts, and a mystical meaning attached to it, by the Christian senator, Cassidorus (480–575) in his *De Artibus et Disciplinis Liberalium Litterarum.* He finds it written in Prov. ix, 1, that 'Wisdom hath builded her house. She hath hewn out her seven pillars.' He concludes that the Seven Liberal Arts are the seven pillars of the house of Wisdom . . ." (*ibid.,* pp. 471–72).

22. Kühnert, *Allgemeinbildung . . .,* p. 24. Cf. Alexandre, *De Congressu . . .* (ed.), pp. 39–40.

23. *Ibid.,* p. 35.

24. Often Philo mentions two or three disciplines, *en passant,* to prove a point quite unrelated to our concerns. Alexandre, *De Congressu . . .* (ed.), pp. 34–35, n. 1, lists some fifteen passages in addition to her main enumerations.

25. Alexandre, *De Congressu . . .* (ed.), p. 43, n. 2, explicitly excludes *Mos.* i.23 from her list of enumerations. The passage in question mentions "arithmetic, geometry, the lore of metre, rhythm and harmony, and the whole subject of music" (*mousikēn tēn sympasan*). The problem, according to Alexandre, is that here music is set "within Egyptian learning, not within the *enkyklios paideia* evoked farther on [at the end of *Mos.* i.23]; this passage reflects more an Alexandrian tradition than a precise program of education." Examining *Mos.* i.23 more closely, we see that music is mentioned in the same breath as arithmetic and geometry. Both of the last-mentioned disciplines are held in good repute as encyclical studies. In my view, there is no basis for disregarding music for having fallen under Egyptian influence while, at the same time, accepting "Chaldaean" astronomy (which we readily do elsewhere).

26. Chadwick in "Philo and the Beginnings of Christian Thought," p. 137, n. 2, states that *Mos.* i.23 "no doubt . . . reflects Philo's own experience when he credits Moses with Greek tutors." Also see C. R. Holladay, *THEIOS ANER in Hellenistic Judaism: A Critique of the Use of This Category in New Testament Christology* (Society of Biblical Literature Dissertation Series 40; Missoula, 1977), pp. 110f.

27. See Alexandre's commentary on this passage in *De Congressu . . .* (ed.), pp. 206–207, n. 2.

28. We shall consider the disciplines (perhaps anachronistically as far as Philo is concerned) according to the *trivium-quadrivium* distinction. Within each group the order used should emphasize similarities between disciplines.

29. The reader is cautioned regarding the word traditionally used to refer to this discipline: "grammar." Grammar as a subject in the ancient world was not a narrow technical subject; it was closer to what we today call "letters." The breadth of the subject as Philo conceived of it is evident in the passages quoted.

30. There are no allusions to grammar in *QE* ii.103 and *Mos.* i.23.

31. Cf. Colson's note in *PLCL* VII, 450. The two parts of grammar, though not explicitly labeled as such, appear in *Agr.* 18. Also see Alexandre, *De Congressu* . . . (ed.), pp. 41–42 and 208, n. 3.

32. *Ibid.,* pp. 56–57.

33. *Ibid.,* p. 57. Here Alexandre refers her readers to Marrou's *History,* pp. 234–35.

34. Cf. *Republic* 607b in which Plato refers to the ancient quarrel between philosophy and poetry. Plato, who himself was gifted with words, had a complex view of poets and poetry, but one of his objections may be seen in the *Republic* 388a–389a.

35. Cf. *Prob.* 98f. and 143.

36. Alexandre, *De Congressu* . . . (ed.), pp. 57–58, also mentions *Mut.* 229. But see *Sac.* 15.

37. *PLCL* IX, 5.

38. See A. D. Nock, "Philo and Hellenistic Philosophy," in *Essays on Religion and the Ancient World,* ed. Z. Stewart (2 vols.; Cambridge, 1972), II, 561–62.

39. Cf. Alexandre, *De Congressu* . . . (ed.), pp. 251–53.

40. *Spec.* i.28–29.

41. It appears in *Cher.* 105; *Agr.* 18; *Som.* i.205; *Cong.* 11,17; and *QG* iii.21.

42. Cf. Clarke, *Higher Education,* pp. 28ff.

43. Colson, *PLCL* V, 604. To this Colson notes an exception: "It is perhaps unusual to find both *taxis* and *oikonomia,* the latter, which covers the management and organization of the material, either superseding the former, or including it as a subdivision." Cf. Alexandre, *De Congressu* . . . (ed.), p. 116, n. 2. Also see George Kennedy, *The Art of Rhetoric in the Roman World* (Princeton, 1972), esp. pp. 114–26.

44. See Robert W. Smith, *The Art of Rhetoric in Alexandria* (The Hague, 1974), Ch. V, esp. pp. 130ff.

45. Cf. *QG* iii.33 and *Agr.* 136 as well as Alexandre, *De Congressu* . . . (ed.), pp. 126–27, n. 1.

46. The reader is referred to J. Drummond, *Philo Judaeus; or, the Jewish-Alexandrian Philosophy in its Development and Completion* (2 vols.; London, 1888), II, 172ff.; E. R. Goodenough, *By Light, Light* (New Haven, 1935), pp. 100–103; Alexandre, *De Congressu* . . . (ed.), p. 116, n. 3; A. Michel, "Quelques aspects de la rhétorique chez Philon," *PAL,* pp. 84ff.

47. Also see *Det.* 127–29 for another formulation of this idea.

48. The term *sophistai* in Philo cannot be relied upon to designate, consistently, practitioners of sophistry. H. A. Wolfson, *Philo* (2 vols.; 4th printing rev.; Cambridge, 1968) I, 59, remarks that *sophistai* may be used in a "laudatory sense of 'sages' and 'experts.' Taken in this sense, it may reflect the Hebrew term *hakamim,* 'sages'. . . ." Colson, "Philo on Education," p. 160, also mentions "a not unfavorable sense" in which the terms *sophistēs* and *sophisteia* are used.

49. Cf. S. Sandmel, *Philo's Place in Judaism: A Study of Conceptions of Abraham in Jewish Literature* (augmented ed.; New York, 1971), p. 156, n. 259.

50. Cf. Philo's reference to "word-catchers and word-traders who greedily stuff themselves with the various opinions that are (found) in the school-studies" (*QG* iii.31).

51. See *Cher.* 8–10, *Sob.* 8–9; also Sandmel, *Philo's Place,* p. 156, n. 258, and p. 162, n. 283.

52. True philosophy leads to virtue; negative philosophy, to sophistry. This is clear from *Post.* 101: "The road leading to Him . . . is also naturally called royal. This road you must take to be philosophy, not the philosophy which is pursued by the sophistic group of present-day people, who, having practiced arts of speech to use against the truth, have given the name of wisdom to their rascality. . . ."

53. See Colson's note *PLCL* IV, 577–78.

54. Cf. *Agr.* 136–43.

55. Philo depicts the sophist as preferring to live a life of petty contentiousness. Cf. *Agr.* 159.

56. Cf. É. Bréhier, *Les idées philosophiques et religieuses de Philon d'Alexandrie* (Paris, 1908), p. 289.

57. Sophists, Philo says in *Mos.* ii.212, "sell their tenets and arguments like any bit of merchandise in the market. . . ." Also see *Post.* 150.

58. Cf. *Cher.* 9.

59. Cf. Bréhier, *Idées,* p. 289.

60. Alexandre, *De Congressu* . . . (ed.), p. 37. Also note her remarks *ibid.,* p. 117, n. 5.

61. Alexandre, "La culture profane . . ." p. 113, tends toward the belief that dialectic and rhetoric are intertwined, for she says that in many texts dialectic appears "liée et confondue avec la rhétorique." All that she proves by the examples in n. 2 (p. 113) is that the two encyclical disciplines coincide in some respects, but by no means in all.

62. The conjunction of dialectic and rhetoric is not original in Philo. Cf. Colson's note to *Cong.* 18, *PLCL* IV, 577. Also see Alexandre, *De Congressu* . . . (ed.), pp. 116–17, n. 4.

63. R. P. McKeon has sought to distinguish between rhetoric and dialectic in Aristotle. Since Philo's distinction, though less rigorous, is similar, the reader may wish to consult McKeon's "Rhetoric and Poetic in the Philosophy of Aristotle," *Aristotle's "Poetics" and English Literature,* ed. E. Olson (Chicago, 1965), pp. 221–22.

64. The translation is by R. D. Hicks for the *LCL.* Also see Diogenes Laertius vii, 46f. and 79.

65. The Stoic division of philosophy into logic, ethics, and physics is reflected in Philo: see, for instance, *Agr.* 15.

66. Alexandre would appear to be wrong on two counts when she states, *De Congressu* . . . (ed.), p. 37, that dialectic in Philo is "one of the parts of philosophy, equivalent to logic." Dialectic is not one of the parts of philosophy; it is an encyclical study. Nor is it equivalent to logic. The philosophical dimension of the encyclia will be discussed at greater length in the following chapter.

67. Kühnert, *Allgemeinbildung . . . ,* pp. 36–37.

68. Goodenough, *Light,* p. 66. Also see Alexandre, *De Congressu* . . . (ed.), pp. 59–60, esp. p. 59, n. 4.

69. *QG* iii.49.

70. Alexandre, *De Congressu* . . . (ed.), p. 208, n. 1.

71. Marrou, *History,* p. 249. On pp. 248–49, Marrou discusses the persistent appearance of aesthetic and moral values in the history of arithmetic.

72. Quoted by F. E. Robbins, "Posidonius and the Sources of Pythagorean Arithmology," *CP* 15 (1920), 309. The definition is that of A. Delatte, "Études sur la littérature pythagoricienne," *Bibl. de l'École des Hautes Études,* fasc. 217 (Paris: 1915), p. 139. This definition is also cited by K. Staehle, *Die Zahlenmystik bei Philon von Alexandreia* (Leipzig, 1931), pp. 2–3. Staehle correctly points to the Pythagorean bias of the definition which must be amended for Philo in that the latter considers numbers over 10. Also see P. Boyancé, "Études philoniennes," *Revue des études grecques* 76 (1963), 82–95.

73. Robbins, "Arithmetic in Philo Judaeus," *CP* 26 (1931), 346. (My emphasis.)

74. *Ibid.,* pp. 349–58.

75. A fuller explanation may be found in É. Herriot, *Philon le Juif: essai sur l'école juive d'Alexandrie* (Paris, 1898), pp. 263–70.

76. Robbins, "The Tradition of Greek Arithmology," *CP* 16 (1921), 102, n. 2, provides a list of some such passages in Philo.

77. One indication of the scope of Philo's arithmetic is Staehle's work, *Die Zahlenmystik . . . ,* as a whole. It gives in arithmetical order a comprehensive list of passages comprising Philo's number symbolism and is an attempt to reconstruct Philo's lost work *Peri Arithmōn.* R. Marcus in "Recent Literature on Philo (1924–1934)," *Jewish Studies in Memory of George A. Kohut* (New York, 1935), p. 475, regards as "plausible" Staehle's contention that there was a handbook of number symbolism which was "the common source of Philo, Varro and Posidonius, and was composed a little before 100 B.C." For the specific passages in Philo which suggest a book on numbers and the probable arithmological nature of the work, also see Robbins, "Arithmetic in Philo Judaeus," p. 359.

78. I should like to express my appreciation to Professor Horst R. Moehring for letting me see his article, "Arithmology as an Exegetical Tool in the Writings of Philo of Alexandria," before its

publication in the Society of Biblical Literature Seminar Papers (ed. P. J. Achtemeier; Missoula, 1978) I, 191–227. Since Moehring's manuscript and my own were evolving at approximately the same time, I was unable to draw more extensively from his work. Yet I would like to cite several sentences from his article which shed light on issues raised in this section: "All this does not mean that arithmology would give unalloyed pleasure to a specialist in pure mathematics. . . . But it does mean that what we have in Philo is a serious attempt to relate the cosmic order to a rational system—expressed in numbers—and thereby to reach an understanding of the universe within thought categories that are available to any and all. It was exactly the mathematically universal character of arithmology which Philo found so attractive for his exegetical work: it could help him to explain the sacred texts of the books of the law in terms that were universally understood, even though not universally accepted" (p. 194).

79. It is omitted in *Agr.* 18 and *QG* iii.21.

80. The first two studies mentioned were grammar and geometry.

81. Alexandre, "La culture profane . . ." pp. 120–21. See *idem, De Congressu . . .* (ed.), pp. 155–56, n. 6. W. Völker, *Fortschritt und Vollendung bei Philo von Alexandrien (Texte und Untersuchungen zur Geschichte der altchristlichen Literatur;* vol. 49, pt. 1; Leipzig, 1938), p. 174, n. 4, also insists that Philo had considerable musical knowledge at his command.

82. According to Liddell and Scott, *hē kanonikē (technē)* refers to the mathematical theory of music based on the division of the monochord (*kanonikos,* of or belonging to a rule). Cf. Alexandre, "La culture profane . . .," p. 121.

83. Marrou, *History,* p. 249, characterizes the discipline as "the science of numerical laws governing music."

84. Alexandre, "La culture profane . . ." p. 120, and *De Congressu . . .* (ed.), pp. 42–43, sees the Philonic discipline in terms of theory. In this she agrees with Marrou, *History,* p. 189.

85. We have already discussed Alexandre's rejection of this passage as non-encyclical, *supra,* n. 25.

86. *Cher.* 93.

87. Philo's picture of the Therapeutae is admittedly idealized. This does not alter the fact that he envisages for them a rich musical life in *Cont.* 29, 80, 84.

88. *The Republic,* trans. P. Shorey (*LCL*).

89. Cf. Colson, "Philo on Education," pp. 154–55, and Alexandre, *De Congressu . . .* (ed.), p. 38.

90. *PLCL* IV, 577.

91. *Institutio Oratoria* I.x.46–49.

92. Drummond, *Philo Judaeus,* I, 263–65. Sandmel, *Philo's Place,* pp. 157–58, n. 261, comments on this passage from Drummond.

93. Drummond's interpretation of *Mig.* 184ff. would be less obscure had he realized that Philo was capable of writing from two distinct vantage points. This will be discussed *infra,* pp. 34, 54.

94. Bréhier, *Idées,* p. 167.

95. Philo goes on to mention various theories concerning the composition of the heavens. See note *PLCL* V, 594.

96. Two other passages which refer to the divinity of the stars are *Opif.* 27, where Philo speaks of heaven as the "most holy dwelling-place of manifest and visible gods" and *Spec.* i.19. On the primacy of the heavens in Philo, see Alexandre, *De Congressu . . .* (ed.), p. 139, n. 3.

97. Wolfson, *Philo,* I, 363; cf. *ibid.,* I, 38.

98. Wolfson makes a valiant attempt to rationalize away the implication of *Gig.* 8, arguing that Philo's "failure to quote it [*Gig.* 8] as the view of somebody else . . . is only an accidental omission" (*Philo,* I, 364). Even if Philo had always been careful to put words about the divinity of the stars in the mouths of others, he might have done so simply out of deference to the opinions of professional astronomers, whose findings he did not necessarily reject.

99. Preconceived notions seem to have forced Wolfson's interpretation here; see my article "A Reappraisal of Wolfson's Method," *SP* 3 (1974-1975), 11-26.

100. Goodenough, *An Introduction to Philo Judaeus* (2nd ed. rev.; Oxford, 1962), pp. 82-83.

101. Holladay, *THEIOS ANER*, p. 180, esp. n. 349, and particularly, pp. 189-94. Holladay's important analysis of the use of *theios* in Philo would indicate that Philo's monotheism is in no way compromised.

102. Cf. *Spec.* iii.1-2, where Philo describes his soul as "a fellow-traveller with the sun and moon and the whole heaven and universe. . . ." Also see *Mig.* 35.

103. This echoes the passage from Plato's *Republic* 529d, quoted at the beginning of the section on astronomy.

104. Cf. *Opif.* 46 and *QG* iv.51.

105. Marrou, *Saint Augustin*, p. 196, esp. n. 4. This semantic situation is discussed, *inter alios*, by Laroche and Pines. E. Laroche, "Les noms grecs de l'astronomie," *Revue de Philologie* 20 (1946), 118-23, claims that it took centuries before men learned in these matters were able to "impose" a distinction between astronomy and astrology on the masses of people. S. Pines, "The Semantic Distinction Between the Terms *Astronomy* and *Astrology* according to Al-Bîrûnî," *Isis* 55 (1964), 343, adds that the two terms were "practically indistinguishable" until the time of Isidore of Seville (d. 636).

106. L. Thorndike, *A History of Magic and Experimental Science* (New York, 1923), I, 353, notes that Philo "believed in much which we should call astrological." Instead of identifying those elements which a modern would call "astrological," we should try to determine what distinctions Philo himself made in the broad spectrum of observations concerning the heavens.

107. Cf. Mayer, *Index Philoneus*.

108. Alexandre, *De Congressu* . . . (ed.), p. 113, n. 4: "The word [*astronomia* in Philo] designates . . . a mixture of knowledge and belief: astronomy, astrology, astral fatalism, and astral religion."

109. In the German translation by Cohn and Heinemann (Breslau, 1909-29) the translators seem to have used the cognate *Astronomie*, thereby avoiding the problem of distinguishing the authentic from the superstitious.

110. Cf. *Abr.* 84: "Now to the meteorologist (*meteōrologikō*) nothing at all seems greater than the universe, and he credits it with the causation of what comes into being."

111. Also see entries under *chaldaizō* and *chaldaioi* in Mayer, *Index Philoneus*.

112. Cf. *Som.* i.53.

113. Cf. *Abr.* 69 and *Cong.* 49.

114. The view that Chaldaea is not used by Philo in a consistently pejorative way is supported by Alexandre, *De Congressu* . . . (ed.), p. 138, n. 1.

115. Philo makes these points succinctly in *Gig.* 62. The passage begins with an association of Chaldaea and *doxa*: "Thus Abraham, while he sojourned in the land of the Chaldaeans— sojourned, that is, in mere opinion (*doxē*). . . ." Since *doxa* is usually construed negatively in Philo, this passage would seem to be an illustration of "Chaldaea" used in a pejorative sense. In the fuller context of Philo's thought, however, a stage of *doxa* must necessarily precede that of coming to knowledge of God. *Doxa* is of the material world and characterizes the beginning of one's migration. The important point here is that Philo concludes *Gig.* 62 with a reminder which puts a positive hue on all the terms associated with migration, both here and in *Heres* 289. Despite his sojourn in Chaldaea, in *Gig.* 62 Philo says that Abraham still was a "man of heaven" (*anthrōpos ouranou*). As we shall see in our consideration of Philo's types of men (*infra*, Ch. 3) this is a technical term of approbation.

116. For instance, in *Heres* 98, Philo speaks of migrations "from astrology to real nature study (*apo astronomias epi physiologian*), from insecure conjecture to firm apprehension (*apo abebaiou eikasias epi pagion katalēpsin*) . . ." In *Heres* 99, Philo mentions "those whose views are of the Chaldaean type," presumably in reference to migrants of the earlier section 98. Does Philo use "Chaldaean"

here in a pejorative way to refer to "astrological" practices as opposed to a more authentic astronomy? I think not. As we shall see in the following chapter, the encyclical studies as a whole may be seen as producing *eikasia*. Here Philo seems to be using "Chaldaean" to distinguish encyclical studies like astronomy proper from higher pursuits. A similar point could be made using *Ebr.* 94. A full explanation of these passages and their contexts depends on discussions of Philonic metaphysics and epistemology.

117. Cf. *Spec.* i.91–92 for another enumeration of events relevant to the study of astronomy.

118. For Stoic influence here see note *PLCL* IV, 565.

119. Cf. Drummond, *Philo Judaeus,* I, 285–87.

120. *QE* ii.109. Cf. *Heres* 176. Also see Colson's note, *PLCL* VIII, 454–55.

121. *Spec.* i.87 and *Mos.* ii.124.

122. Goodenough, *Light,* pp. 99–100 and 209–10.

123. F. Cumont, *Astrology and Religion among the Greeks and Romans,* American Lectures on the History of Religions, Series of 1911–1912 (New York, 1912), pp. 32–33.

124. Philo makes this clear in *Spec.* i.13f. Also see Sandmel, *Philo's Place,* p. 158, n. 261: "Philo seems to have believed that the stars could foretell, *Mos.* ii.126; *LA* i.8; and *Opif.* 58. But there is a difference between the ability to foretell and the ability to control. Ascription of ruling power to the stars would be to Philo atheism."

Bréhier, *Idées,* pp. 180ff., correctly states Philo's belief that since all things are possible for God, God alone can know the future. Yet God's exclusive knowledge of the future does not apply to events indicated by the stars, for such knowledge he shares with men.

125. Cumont, *Astrology and Religion . . .,* p. 28.

126. Wolfson, *Philo,* I, 329. In this passage Wolfson is citing *Heres* 300–301. Philo's terms are *heimarmenē* (fate) and *anankē* (necesity). Wolfson points out that in *Mig.* 179 Philo accuses the Chaldaeans of having made fate and necessity into gods. Cf. D. Amand, *Fatalisme et liberté dans l'antiquité grecque* (Louvain, 1945), p. 85.

127. Drummond, *Philo Judaeus,* I, 348, argues that Philo *assumes* free will "as a fact, just as unquestionable as our possession of reason. . . ." If this is an accurate assessment—and I think it is—we should not be surprised that Philo fails to *prove* the falsity of determinism. Cf. *Immut.* 47–51.

128. P. Wendland, *Philos Schrift über die Vorsehung* (Berlin, 1892), pp. 24ff., gives an account of Philo's decisive rejection of Stoic fatalism. By drawing absurd or unacceptable implications of determinism, Philo discredits the "opinion that attributes all acts of men to the constellations in the period of their birth" (Wendland, p. 24).

129. Cf. Wolfson, *Philo,* I, 176–77.

130. Cf. *Mig.* 179.

131. Goodenough, *Light,* pp. 111–12.

CHAPTER 2

1. For a general introduction, see J. Bowen, *A History of Western Education* (2 vols.; New York, 1972), I, 152–66 and 220–34.

2. A. J. Festugière, *Revue des études grecques* 52 (1939), 239.

3. Marrou, *History,* p. 528, n. 2.

4. Wolfson, *Philo,* I, 81.

5. Wolfson's reasons for doubting the validity of Philo's personal testimony are rooted in his concept of Native Judaism. I discuss this general problem in "Reappraisal of Wolfson's Method," pp. 11ff.

6. In *Cong.* 73, immediately before the passage cited in the text above, Philo says that "personal experience (*martys d' ho peponthōs*) will prove the most infallible of testimonies." Then *Cong.* 74

begins in an emphatic mode: *egō goun*. Both A. W. Argyle, "The Ancient University of Alexandria," *Classical Journal* 69 (1974), 349, and Alexandre, *De Congressu* . . . (ed.), p. 41, take Philo's testimony to be true.

7. Josephus, for instance, in his *Vita* 7–12 says that he passed through the courses of the Pharisees, Sadducees, and Essenes. We might have difficulty imagining in what institutional context Josephus did this, but we do not doubt that his education included some introduction to each of the groups mentioned.

8. Cf. Goodenough, *Introduction*, p. 46.

9. S. Belkin, *Philo and the Oral Law* (Cambridge, 1940), p. 23.

10. It should not be forgotten that the institutions discussed in this chapter were funded privately; cf. Smith, *The Art of Rhetoric*, pp. 110–12.

11. See L. Massebieau and É. Bréhier, "Essai sur la chronologie de la vie et des oeuvres de Philon," *Revue de l'histoire des religions* 53 (1906), 29–31; Goodenough, *The Politics of Philo Judaeus* (New Haven, 1938), pp. 64–66, and *Introduction*, pp. 2–3; J. Daniélou, *Philon d'Alexandrie* (Paris, 1958), pp. 13–14; Dillon, *Middle Platonists*, p. 139; and S. S. Foster, "A Note on the 'Note' of J. Schwarz," *SP* 4 (1976–77), 25–32.

12. Sandmel, *Philo's Place*, p. 136.

13. See Goodenough, *The Jurisprudence of the Jewish Courts in Egypt* (New Haven, 1929), pp. 52–53.

14. *CPJ*, I, 51–52. On the economic diversification of the Jews of Roman Egypt, also see L. Fuchs, *Die Juden Aegyptens in ptolemäischer und römischer Zeit* (Wien, 1924), pp. 48ff.

15. *CPJ*, I, 52 (in reference to papyri nos. 146–47); also see Tcherikover, *Hellenistic Civilization and the Jews* (trans. S. Applebaum; Philadelphia, 1959), pp. 333ff.

16. *CPJ*, I, 50. Cf. Salo W. Baron, *A Social and Religious History of the Jews: Ancient Times* (2d ed. rev.; Philadelphia, 1952), I, 264–67, 281.

17. A. H. M. Jones, *The Cities of the Eastern Roman Provinces* (Oxford, 1971), p. 308. In addition to the cost of membership, there were other fees which even the wealthy found onerous.

18. Cf. Plutarch, *De liberis educandis* 8E, which also indicates that a proper education might be beyond the means of the common people.

19. Tcherikover, "Jewish Apologetic Literature Reconsidered," *Eos* 48 (1956), 191f. Cf. Hengel, *Judaism and Hellenism*, I, 299.

20. Tcherikover also discusses the question of a lower-class ideology in *CPJ*, I, 47, 67–68, 74–75. Without strictly identifying Tcherikover's lower classes with the conservative Jews depicted in M. J. Shroyer, "Alexandrian Jewish Literalists," *JBL* 55 (1936), 261–84, I would suggest that there are interesting parallels.

21. The picture which emerges from Philo is similar to that presented by Sarah B. Pomeroy for Athenian women in *Goddesses, Whores, Wives, and Slaves: Women in Classical Antiquity* (London, 1976), p. 74. Lieberman's opposing view, in his "Response," *Proceedings of the Rabbinical Assembly of America* 12 (1949), 279–80, is not convincing, at least for upper-class Alexandria of the first century.

22. H. Box, *Philonis Alexandrini: In Flaccum* (London, 1939), p. 107.

23. R. A. Baer, Jr., *Philo's Use of the Categories Male and Female* (Leiden, 1970), p. 40.

24. *Ibid.*, p. 41.

25. I. Heinemann, *Philons griechische und jüdische Bildung* (Breslau, 1932), p. 235, remarks that Musonius and Ben Asai proposed the education of women.

26. *Ibid.*, pp. 235–36. Cf. W. A. Meeks, "The Image of the Androgyne: Some Uses of a Symbol in Earliest Christianity," *History of Religions* 13 (1974), 165–80. Also see N. Drazin, *The History of Jewish Education from 515 B.C.E. to 220 C.E.*, John Hopkins University Studies in Education, Vol. 29 (Baltimore, 1940), pp. 124ff., and N. Morris, *The Jewish School* (London, 1937), pp. 29ff.

27. Hengel, *Judaism and Hellenism*, I, 66. Also see *CPJ*, I, 38–39.

28. Wolfson, *Philo*, I, 79. See Marrou's remarks on the ephebea in his *History*, esp. pp. 153ff. In

my discussion of Greek institutions of higher learning, I shall refer for the most part to the gymnasium. The word *ephēbeia* does not appear in Philo; activities which seem to have occurred in the gymnasium are mentioned, as in *Spec.* ii.98.

29. Hengel, *Judaism and Hellenism*, I, 65–66, presents a brief history of barbarian involvement in Greek culture. Cf. M. P. Nilsson, *Die hellenistische Schule* (München, 1955), pp. 85ff.

30. Jones, *Cities*, pp. 308–309. Also see T. A. Brady, "The Gymnasium in Ptolemaic Egypt," *University of Missouri Studies* 11 (1936), 16ff.

31. Hengel, *Judaism and Hellenism*, I, 66.

32. Tcherikover, *Hellenistic Civilization*, p. 311. Cf. S. Applebaum, "The Legal Status of the Jewish Communities in the Diaspora," *Compendia Rerum Iudaicarum ad Novum Testamentum*, eds. S. Safrai and M. Stern (Assen, 1974), I, esp. 434ff.

33. Cf. *CPJ*, I, 60–62.

34. *CPJ* No. 151 = vol. II, 29–33.

35. Cf. translator's notes on this passage in *PLCL* I, 412, and Peder Borgen, *Bread from Heaven* (Leiden, 1965), pp. 123ff. The passage *LA* iii.167–68 is discussed more fully below, pp. 44–45.

36. *CPJ* No. 153 (= vol. II, 43).

37. Feldman, "The Orthodoxy of the Jews in Hellenistic Egypt," *Jewish Social Studies* 22 (1960), 224–25. For references to the tutelary deities of the gymnasia, see P. M. Fraser, *Ptolemaic Alexandria* (3 vol.; Oxford, 1972), II, 353, n. 149. Also see Townsend, "Ancient Education . . ." p. 149.

38. These passages are discussed in my "Reappraisal of Wolfson's Method," pp. 12ff. Cf. Testament of Abraham (Recension A) 10.2, in the forthcoming Doubleday edition by E. P. Sanders.

39. *PLCL* IV, 198.

40. Marrou, *History*, p. 158.

41. Feldman, "Orthodoxy," p. 225.

42. On the length of Jewish settlement in Egypt and Alexandria in particular, see *CPJ*, I, 1–4. Goodenough's *Jurisprudence of the Jewish Courts in Egypt* is an attempt to demonstrate the judicial aspects of the code which Alexandrian Jews developed. I am suggesting that there was a similar religious code which guided Philo's colleagues in the business of accommodating themselves spiritually to their surroundings. For other instances of accommodation see Fraser, *Ptolemaic Alexandria*, I, 282–84. Lieberman, "Response," p. 277, makes a relevant point: "The character of the Alexandrian Jews was not much different from that of the Alexandrian Gentiles. The Alexandrians were notorious at that time for their short temper, their boisterousness, their seditious character, their harshness and their sharpness. The occasional remarks found in the Talmud about the Alexandrian Jews bear out this record."

43. Hengel, *Judaism and Hellenism*, I, 68; also see *ibid.*, p. 299.

44. *Mos.* ii.216 contains another relevant phrase; on Sabbaths, Philo says, the Jews studied "the truths of nature" (*theōria tōn peri physin*). This phrase, which also appears in *Dec.* 98 in conjunction with Sabbath study, has been interpreted variously. Colson in *PLCL* VI, 556, takes it to mean "theology." Wolfson, *Philo*, I, 79, interprets it as "problems of general philosophy." J. S. Boughton, in his unpublished dissertation "The Idea of Progress in Philo Judaeus" (Columbia University, 1932), pp. 79–80, suggests that the passage refers to the study of "what ought to be done and said" in particular cases. These commentators appear to agree that Sabbaths were not devoted to encyclical study.

45. Cf. *Mut.* 256–60 and the discussion of this passage in P. Borgen, *Bread from Heaven* (Leiden, 1965), pp. 111ff., esp. Borgen's criticism of Colson's note in *PLCL* V, 274–75.

46. Philo's characterization of the encyclia will be discussed in detail in the following section.

47. Cf. Alexandre, *De Congressu* . . . (ed.), pp. 45–46.

48. Feldman, "Orthodoxy," pp. 222–23.

49. Cf. *supra*, p. 5. Also see *QG* iii.43: "Skill in the study of astronomy is acquired in one part of the world, (namely) in the heaven and in the revolutions and circlings of the stars, whereas wis-

dom (pertains) to the nature of all things, both sense-perceptible and intelligible" (= *PLCL* Supp. I, 235).

50. Baer, *Philo's Use of the Categories . . .*, p. 89.

51. *Ibid.*, p. 91.

52. *Ibid.*, p. 95.

53. For instance, Goodenough notes in *Light*, p. 247, that *Heres* reflects an ideal, while "the next treatise, the *de Congressu*, begins at the bottom" in an attempt to present essentially the same process. Called upon to explain how Philo could depict certain distinctions as "superfluous refinements" in one passage (*Agr.* 140–41) and as "true philosophy" in another (*Cong.* 149), Colson speaks of "Philo's capacity for looking at things from opposite points of view" (see *PLCL* IV, 537). As divine wisdom comes closer to the aspiring man, that man's opinions change, sometimes radically. Philo, himself an aspiring man, reflects this process in his own works.

54. Cf. H. Jonas, *Gnosis und spätantiker Geist,* Pt. II, i (2d ed. rev.; Göttingen, 1966), p. 76.

55. Commentators agree that sensation, per se, is not evil in Philo. For instance Drummond, *Philo Judaeus*, II, 300, says "Philo expressly declares [in *LA* iii.67] that sensation cannot be classed with things either morally bad or morally good, but, being common to the wise man and the fool, occupies an intermediate position, and becomes bad in the fool and good in the virtuous." Thus, too, Baer, *Philo's Use of the Categories . . .*, p. 92: "*Aisthēsis* is frequently referred to in highly pejorative terms, but it is never held to be inherently or absolutely evil."

56. The same sentinent is expressed in *Post.* 137: "She who belongs to the band of devotees of school-learning (*tē men tois paideumasi tois enkykliois <en>choreuousē*) needs, as it were, certain bodily vessels of sense-perception—eyes, ears—for the acquirement of the results of study. . . ." Also see *Cong.* 155.

57. Cf. Wolfson, *Philo*, II, 3–4: "With regard to the dependence of reason upon sensation, [Philo] says that it is impossible to apprehend the intelligible world or any other existing being which is incorporeal 'except by making corporeal objects our starting point' [*Som.* i.187]."

58. In the paragraphs to follow, it will become clearer that *mesos* describes the encyclia quite aptly and that it is an appropriate term to be used in synonyms for the disciplines: e.g., *mesē paideia* (cf. *supra*, p. 3).

59. Wolfson, *Philo*, II, 7 (pp. 3–11 for the extended argument).

60. This issue was first raised in connection with the limits of the disciplines, *supra*, p. 5.

61. The movement from astronomy to philosophy, through the agency of sight, is also depicted in *Spec.* iii.187ff. and *Abr.* 158–64. The source of these passages is the *Timaeus* 47a, b.

62. The same definition of wisdom is given in *QG* iii.43. What Philo means by "divine" may be seen later in the same section: "Not only to see all substances and natures but also to trace and search out their various causes shows a power that is more perfect than is human" (=*PLCL* Supp. I, 236). Cf. Dillon, *Middle Platonists*, p. 141.

63. On the question of the point of transition from arts and sciences to philosophy proper, see Plato's *Republic* vii.524ff., *Philebus* 56d–59b, and Seneca's *Epistle* 88. 24–28. Also see Lodge, *Plato's Theory of Education*, pp. 27–28.

64. Cf. *Republic* vii.529c-d. Also see G. desJardins, "How to Divide the Divided Line," *Review of Metaphysics* 29 (1976), 483–96.

65. Cf. *Sob.* 9. Also see Henrichs, "Philosophy, the Handmaiden . . ." pp. 444–45.

66. Y. Amir, "Philo and the Bible," *SP* 2 (1973), 6, points to some of the difficulties in maintaining an intermediate position between truth and its opposite. Cf. A. A. Long, "Language and Thought in Stoicism," *Problems in Stoicism*, ed. A. A. Long (London, 1971), p. 101.

67. See Colson's note regarding the translation of these words in *PLCL* IV, 530–31. The alternative rendering does not alter the point being made here.

68. The opposition between conjecture and truth is clear in Philo: "There is a natural hostility between conjecture and truth (*stochasmos alētheia*), between vanity and knowledge, and between the

divination which has no true inspiration and sound sober wisdom" (*Conf.* 159). "The human mind in its blindness does not perceive its real interest and all it can do is to take conjecture and guesswork (*eikasia kai stochasmō*) for its guide instead of knowledge" (*Legat.* 21). Also see *Spec.* iv.50 and *Ebr.* 167. In this discussion, we are naturally talking about human truth. There are, of course, divine matters concerning which neither philosophers nor sages will know the truth; cf. *Opif.* 72.

69. In *Opif.* 58, Philo says that on the basis of movements of the heavenly bodies "men conjecture (*stochazontai*) future issues. . . ." The choice of this verb, denoting lack of certainty, is consistent with Philo's usage elsewhere. Cf. *Spec.* i.38.

70. We may quote with profit a passage from Plato's *Timaeus*. Even though Philo did not consider the encyclia simply as a "pastime," the distinctions made by Plato apply to our author: "When a man, for the sake of recreation, lays aside discourse about eternal things and gains an innocent pleasure from the consideration of such plausible accounts of becoming, he will add to his life a sober and sensible pastime" (*Timaeus* 59c-d, trans. F. M. Cornford).

71. Cf. Colson's note in *PLCL* IV, 580. Also see Heinemann, *Philons griechische und jüdische Bildung*, pp. 433-34, and Dillon, *Middle Platonists*, p. 145.

72. See H. Baumgarten, "Vitam brevem esse, longam artem," *Gymnasium* 77 (1970), 299-323.

73. See Colson's note, *PLCL* V, 299. *Som.* i.8ff., as well as several other passages discussed below, are mentioned by Marcus, "Outline of Philo's System of Education," pp. 229-30.

74. Colson's note, *PLCL* V, 591: "For this 'recognized formula of the Platonic school' *cf.* particularly *Philebus* 14C, 15B ff."

75. Cf. H. Guyot, *L'Infinité divine depuis Philon le Juif jusqu'à Plotin* (Paris, 1906), pp. 80-81. Also see R. Williamson, *Philo and the Epistle to the Hebrews* (Leiden, 1970), p. 284.

76. E.g., *Opif.* 10-11.

77. Cf. Wolfson, *Philo*, II, 4-5.

78. "God has bestowed no gift of grace (*kecharistai*) on Himself, for He does not need it, but He has given the world to the world, and its parts to themselves and to each other . . . But He has given His good things in abundance to the All and its parts, not because He judged anything worthy of grace (*axion charitos*), but looking to His eternal goodness, and thinking that to be beneficient was incumbent on His blessed and happy nature" (*Immut.* 107-8).

79. Cf. *LA* i.34. Also see B. E. Schein, "Our Father Abraham" (unpublished diss., Yale University, 1972), pp. 34f.

80. This explanation of differences between individuals is consistent with Philo's more general explanation of how evil originated in the world. Cf., for instance, *Opif.* 23. In other passages, Philo reiterates his belief that man's God-given receptivity varies greatly: "It is the nature of some souls to be always childish" (*Fug.* 146); some men have an "incapacity for instruction or indifference to learning" (*Decal.* 59). Concerning men of such an unreceptive mold, Philo writes: "Those who have studied the lower subjects, but have been unable through dullness of nature to imbibe any knowledge, will deserve praise if they abandon them. . . . If . . . our nature opposes our efforts for progress in them, let us not fruitlessly resist her" (*Sac.* 116-17). Also see *Spec.* i.43.

81. Cf. Colson's note, *PLCL* IX, 186. The textual difficulties here do not alter the point which this passage illustrates.

82. On the superiority of the teacher, see *QG* iv.104: "The pupil's capacity to learn is not like the teacher's capacity to teach, since the one is perfect, and the other imperfect."

83. *Spec.* iv.140: "If some less courageous spirit hesitates through modesty and is slow to come near to learn, that teacher should go himself and pour into his ears . . . a continuous flood of instruction. . . ." Also see *QE* ii.25.

84. Cf. Clark, *Higher Education*, pp. 1-2, esp. n. 1, for further discussion of septennial schemes in antiquity.

85. Another account of the ages of man, given in *Opif.* 105, is based on Hippocrates' conception and is even less helpful than Solon's in indicating when the encyclia might be studied. A third

account of the ages of man (*LA* i.10) is incomplete insofar as it details only three hebdomads. Also see *Jos.* 127. Marrou discusses the matter in *History,* pp. 147–48.

86. Since these passages are not part of the celebration of the number seven, unlike *Opif.* 103–104, the heptad does not play a significant role. Only the first period, childhood, is seven years in length (*Heres* 294).

87. Cf. R. Marcus, "Outline of Philo's System of Education," p. 224, in which it is pointed out that Jewish scholars had traditionally spoken of only three periods of a man's life: namely, childhood, youth, and old age.

88. Cf. Alexandre, *De Congressu* . . . (ed.), pp. 159–60, n. 4, on the natural implantation of the passions in the soul.

89. Some other passages in which Philo mentions pedagogues: *Sac.* 15; *Leg.* 115; *Mig.* 116; and *Spec.* ii.233. These references may be a reflection of one aspect of Philo's own education and an indication of his social position. Cf. Marrou, *History,* p. 206.

90. The main exceptions to this would appear to be Moses and Isaac. Regarding the former, in *Mos.* i.25, Philo makes a special point of saying that despite temptation, Moses "did not, as some, allow the lusts of adolescence to go unbridled." Also see Alexandre, *De Congressu* . . . (ed.), p. 160, n. 1.

91. In Philo, the number ten is "sacred to education" (*Sac.* 122). The reader is referred to Colson's note on this passage: *PLCL* II, 491–92. Also see Alexandre, *De Congressu* . . . (ed.), pp. 242–44. Philo cites the biblical verse (Gen. 16.3) in *Cong.* 71.

92. Prof. S. Daniel has suggested to me that the instrumental sense of this *en* should be made more clear than the Loeb translation makes it.

93. Commenting on *Prob.* 160, Williamson, *Philo and the Epistle to the Hebrews,* pp. 283–84, says that the process of pre-education and education is divided into three stages: "the 'milk' stage, the 'soft food' stage, and the 'hard food' stage. . . . The 'milk' stage is the pre-educative period, the 'soft food' stage is the period of ordinary education, the Encyclia, consisting of literature, rhetoric, mathematics, music and logic. The 'meat' stage is the process of enlightenment in the realm of philosophical truth." Although Philo is not always consistent in his treatment of these themes, *Prob.* 160 fits reasonably well into Philo's four ages of man. (Presumably in this scheme the "milk" stage is adolescence.) For our purposes it is important to note the pre-educational stage *prior* to the encyclia.

94. We may arrive at this conclusion from internal evidence by adding seven years of childhood and the ten years of adolescence just discussed. Significantly and, I dare say, not coincidentally, Hengel, *Hellenism and Judaism,* I, 66, places gymnasium education at the same juncture of a man's life: "Instruction in the 'Greek school' was presumably divided into three age groups: school age from about 7 to 14/15, followed by the period of the ephebate which lasted one or two years, which was the real time of training in the gymnasium, dominated above all by physical exercise and also a degree of military training. This was in turn followed by the stage of the 'young men,' who continued their instruction in the gymnasium until about the age of twenty." Hengel then goes on to discuss grammar, which youths of 16 or 17 presumably would have studied after the ephebate. For Philo, this was the beginning of an encyclical curriculum; cf. *Cong.* 74–76.

The issue concerning the age at which one entered the *ephēbeia* has been discussed in Nilsson, *Die hellenistische Schule*; Marrou took issue with Nilsson on this point. The state of the debate between Nilsson and Marrou is summarized by Townsend, "Ancient Education . . ." p. 160, n. 56: "There is some dispute about the age that one entered the Hellenistic *ephēbeia.* Nilsson, pp. 34–42, argues against Marrou that the term *ephēboi* must refer to boys in their early teens. Marrou, in his review of Nilsson (*L'antiquité classique* 25 [1956], 234–240), answers his arguments in detail and also gives some new evidence that *ephēboi* refers to an older age group."

95. Colson, "Philo on Education," p. 157. Alexandre, *De Congressu* . . . (ed.), p. 44, n. 2, agrees with this chronology, pointing to the influence of Plato.

96. Alexandre, *ibid.,* pp. 49–50, says that age is the main factor in moving from secular education to the fourth stage of life, Wisdom. I disagree. To attain a proper age is an important condition, but it is not sufficient. One still has to be the right type of man (cf. *ibid.,* p. 50, n. 1). Also see *ibid.,* pp. 107–8, n. 4.

97. Women, in Philo's view, were incapable of attaining spiritual maturity.

98. This is Philo's term in *Heres* 298 for the fourth stage or the "fourth generation within the soul."

99. Cf. *Post.* 138 and Goodenough, *Light,* pp. 157ff.

100. Marcus' reconstruction: *tēs paideias, PLCL* Supp. I, 438, n. *h.*

101. Philo's concern with specific difficulties arising from the improper study of the encyclia suggests that there actually were students of the disciplines.

102. Cf. *Cong.* 126: "The art or science (*technē*) that is studied does seize and take hold of the learner and persuades him to be her lover."

103. Colson, "Philo on Education," p. 156, notes: "The Encyclia as a whole had for a widespread public a charm and romance which they have now for only a few." Also see Alexandre, *De Congressu . . .* (ed.), pp. 76–77.

104. Cf. Alexandre's commentary, *ibid.,* p. 157, as well as Colson's, *PLCL* IV, 578.

105. The same thought is expressed in *Sac.* 44.

106. Cf. *LA* iii.228–29: "If we repose our trust in our own reasonings, we shall construct and build up the city of Mind that corrupts the truth. . . . To trust God is a true teaching, but to trust our vain reasonings is a lie." Goodenough, *Light,* p. 125, correctly refers to these people as "rationalists." Also see *LA* ii.46.

107. This passage is noted in Goodenough, *Light,* p. 171, and Wolfson, *Philo,* I, 54–55. Also see Marcus, "Outline of Philo's System of Education," p. 228.

108. A word about sanctions is in order. Williamson, *Philo and the Epistle to the Hebrews,* p. 303; T. H. Billings, *The Platonism of Philo Judaeus* (Chicago, 1919), pp. 86–87; and Marcus, "Outline of Philo's System of Education," p. 226, acknowledge punishment as a part of Philo's educational system. Also see, Alexandre, *De Congressu . . .* (ed.), pp. 61 and 254–56. In the latter, note in particular Alexandre's remark, based on *Immut.* 51–54, that correction is essentially the work of God. On the linguistic connection between education and corporal punishment (with no explicit reference to Philo) see Marrou, *History,* p. 221.

109. Cf. Colson's summary of Philo's views on the appropriate time to study the encyclia in *PLCL* III, 502.

110. Drummond, *Philo Judaeus,* II, 306.

111. *Ibid.*

112. Cf. my discussion of this passage, *supra,* p. 30, where *LA* iii.167 is quoted at greater length. Also see translator's note, *PLCL* I, 412–13.

113. Borgen, *Bread,* pp. 123–24.

114. *Ibid.*

115. *Ibid.,* p. 125.

116. Cf. E. R. Goodenough, *The Politics of Philo Judaeus* (New Haven, 1938), esp. chaps. I–III.

117. We should remember that the study of history and poetry belongs specifically to the higher stage of the curriculum in grammar, *grammatikē*; cf. *supra,* pp. 5–6.

118. Alexandre, *De Congressu . . .* (ed.), p. 54, sees in *Sac.* 78 the obligation of the *sage* to conform in his public life. One would surely expect this of a sage. I would suggest that *Sac.* 78 likewise applies to those who never attain perfect virtue. See the following chapter for a discussion of the sage and other mortals.

119. This phrase is a fine example of Philo's use of "choric terminology," as de Rijk notes in *"Enkyklios Paideia,"* pp. 77ff.; cf. *supra,* p. 3.

120. The encyclia are also related to custom in *Sob.* 38; note the substitution of *nomimos* for *mathēsis* in the modified form of the educational triad.

121. Translator's note here: "or 'be convicted as incapable of doing service,'" *PLCL* III, 349.

122. Cf. *Mig.* 88: "Fair fame is won as a rule by all who cheerfully take things as they find them and interfere with no established customs, but maintain with care the constitution of their country."

123. Cf. *Mos.* ii.211.

CHAPTER 3

1. In his article "Freedom and Determinism in Philo of Alexandria," *SP* 3, 52, D. Winston uses this passage to advance the hypothesis that Philo employs a concept of relative, rather than absolute, free will. Our study will corroborate Winston's conclusion.

2. Cf. *Rep.* iv.

3. Long, "Language and Thought in Stoicism," p. 101. D. Tsekourakis, *Studies in the Terminology of Early Stoic Ethics, Hermes: Zeitschrift für klassische Philologie, Heft* 32 (Wiesbaden, 1974), has refined this viewpoint, arguing that not every action of the sage must reflect his role as *sophos*. "Even the sage," Tsekourakis contends, p. 10, "can have his human nature as a guide in his acts in common life, provided that it is not in disagreement with the universal nature and *orthos logos.*" Also see *ibid.,* pp. 124ff., on the general characteristics of the sage.

4. Long, "Language and Thought in Stoicism," p. 101.

5. Dillon, *Middle Platonists,* pp. 77–78; cf. Long, *Hellenistic Philosophy,* p. 206.

6. J. M. Rist, *Stoic Philosophy* (Cambridge, 1969), pp. 22ff. Also see J. Dillon and A. Terian, "Philo and the Stoic Doctrine of *Eupatheiai,*" *SP* 4 (1976–77), 17–24.

7. Rist, *Stoic Philosophy,* p. 90.

8. I am especially grateful for the remarks by Professor David Winston on this subject in Colloquy 15, *"General Education" in Philo of Alexandria,* The Center for Hermeneutical Studies in Hellenistic and Modern Culture (Berkeley, 1975), p. 42. (Bibliographical entry under T. Conley.) Winston refers readers to G. Stählin's article on *prokopē, TDNT* 6, 703–11. A passage from this article (p. 706) may be quoted here with profit: *"Prokopē* plays a significant role in the system of Stoic ethics. It denotes the way from *aphrosynē* to *sophia* (cf. Chrysipp. Fr., 425 [v. Arnim, III, 104, 18]), from *kakia* to *aretē* (Fr., 217 [III, 51, 37]; Fr. 530 [III, 142, 17f.]; Fr., 532 [III, 142, 33f.]), and hence from *kakodaimonia* to *eudaimonia* (cf. Epict. *Diss.,* I, 4, 3). This is the only *prokopē* of real value, Epict. *Diss.,* I, 4, 5. Yet in ancient Stoicism it is reckoned only among the *mesa* (cf. Chrysipp. Fr., 538 [v. Arnim, III, 143, 35f.]), the so-called intermediate virtues. . . ."

9. Trans. by R. M. Gummere in *LCL* (London, 1925), vol. III.

10. I. G. Kidd, "Stoic Intermediaries and the End for Man," *Problems in Stoicism* (ed. Long), p. 164.

11. *Ibid.,* p. 165.

12. Rist, *Stoic Philosophy,* p. 90.

13. Stählin, *prokopē, TDNT* 6, 706.

14. Rist, *Stoic Philosophy,* p. 91.

15. Referring to the Stoa, D. L. Tiede, *The Charismatic Figure as Miracle Worker,* Society of Biblical Literature Dissertation Series, No. 1 (Missoula, 1972), p. 55, says: "The fact that the true sage is something of an unattainable ideal does not diminish his paradigmatic value."

16. Wolfson, *Philo,* I, 366–70; so too Sandmel, *Philo's Place,* p. 158, n. 263.

17. *PLCL* IV, 306–307.

18. This man is familiar to us as the generic man of the first creation in *Opif.* 69ff. Also see Sandmel, *Philo's Place,* p. 161, esp. n. 274. (The reference to Drummond in n. 274 should read II, 275ff., *q.v.*)

19. Cf. L. K. K. Dey, *The Intermediary World and Patterns of Perfection in Philo and Hebrews,* Society of Biblical Literature Dissertation Series, No. 25 (Missoula, 1975), pp. 38–39.

20. Baer, *Philo's Use of the Categories Male and Female,* pp. 81–82, n. 1, notes that several of Philo's statements about types of men cannot be correlated. As long as students of Philo expect consistent terminology, the problem of types of men in Philo will remain confused. I would suggest that we not try to reconcile, for instance, the "heavenly" man of *QG* i.93 with the "heavenly" man of *LA* i.31. Philo's terminology *is* ambivalent; his concepts of classes, however, usually are not. Consequently, we should see how Philo conceives of each "heavenly" man in context, developing our conception of Philonic classifications of men without regard to the names he uses in particular instances.

21. Cf. *Mut.* 24: "It is His will that the wicked man (*phaulon*) should be under His sway as his Lord (*kyriou*) . . .; that the man of progress (*prokoptonta*) should be benefited by Him as God (*theou*) and thus through those kindnesses reach perfection; that the perfect (*teleion*) should be guided by Him as Lord (*kyriou*) and benefited by Him as God (*theou*). . . ." In this passage, these features are noteworthy: (a) the tripartite division of men, (b) the use of the term *prokoptonta* for men of the middle classification, (c) the assumption that a man of progress can reach perfection, and (d) the mobility of the classes. Also see Dillon's comments on *Fug.* 97ff. in *Middle Platonists,* p. 169.

22. Even Moses who is, from the start, a man of God studied the encyclia; cf. *Mos.* i.23 and Holladay's remarks on this subject in *THEIOS ANER,* p. 111.

23. On the ethical dimension of Philo's terminology, see Holladay, *ibid.,* pp. 129–30, esp. at n. 155. *Abr.* 122–25 makes a similar division of men according to three temperaments.

24. Cf. *Plant.* 14; also see U. Früchtel, *Die kosmologischen Vorstellungen bei Philo von Alexandrien* (Leiden, 1968), pp. 62ff.

25. Cf. A. O. Lovejoy, *The Great Chain of Being: A Study of the History of an Idea* (New York, 1960), p. 54; and F. Keferstein, *Philo's Lehre von den göttlichen Mittelwesen* (Leipzig, 1846), pp. 1–25 and 226–56. (In the former section, Keferstein discusses the necessity of divine *Mittelwesen*; in the latter, angels specifically.)

26. Holladay, *THEIOS ANER,* p. 172.

27. Dey, *Intermediary World,* pp. 56–57, contains a discussion of this passage. There is a parallel between the small number of Philo's God-born men on earth and the number of bona fide Stoic sages.

28. *Ibid.,* p. 40, gives these and other appellations. Sandmel, *Philo's Place,* pp. 178–79, n. 348, observes that "in Philo's writings expressions such as, son of God, friend of God, family of God, and prophet are nearly interchangeable." These expressions, as well as terms used in *Som.* ii. 229–37 and *Praem.* 43–44 should be noted.

29. Tsekourakis, *Studies in the Terminology of Early Stoic Ethics,* p. 136.

30. Cf. Goodenough, *Light,* pp. 153–57. On Philo's concept of the sage, also see U. Wilckens' article on *sophia, TDNT,* 7, 500.

31. For a sense of the necessity of divine grace, see Wolfson, *Philo,* I, 446–49. Wolfson seems to think that one can secure divine help by doing specific things. My sense of the relevant passages in Philo is that the entire process is incalculable. Cf. *ibid.,* pp. 163–64.

32. Goodenough, *Light,* p. 74.

33. Goodenough remarks, *ibid.,* p. 89, that Moses had this quality "to a degree that completely surpassed the rest." Cf. W. A. Meeks, *The Prophet King: Moses Traditions and the Johannine Christology* (Leiden, 1967), p. 110.

34. Dey, *Intermediary World,* p. 64, argues convincingly that Moses stands closest "in terms of a hierarchy of proximities to God." Dey, *ibid.,* pp. 64–65, cites *Post.* 76–78 which conjoins Isaac and Moses (self-taught and self-learnt wisdom) and contrasts them with Abraham and Jacob (men who progress and become better through practice). Also see M. Braun, *History and Romance in Graeco-Oriental Literature* (Oxford, 1938), pp. 26–31.

35. Cf. Holladay, *THEIOS ANER,* pp. 118–21 and 132ff.

36. Holladay's analysis of this passage, *ibid.,* pp. 138–41, supplements our picture of Moses, the *sophos.* Holladay's reexamination of the concept *theios anēr* is most welcome. Passages which

previously had been cited to bolster the *theios anēr* theme in Philo may now be read, in the light of Holladay's analysis, as passages which simply elaborate the virtues of God-born *men*. For instance, I agree with Meeks, *Prophet-King*, p. 105, that Philo's descriptions of Moses' assumption "clearly depict the apotheosis of a divine *man*, not the return of an incarnate deity, as Good-enough suggests." Tiede's analysis of *Sac.* 8 in *Charismatic Figure*, p. 125, seems incorrect; I do not think there is sufficient evidence to warrant calling Moses divine. It is also an error to consider Moses' presence "inferior in degree only" to God (*ibid.*, p. 132). Moses' virtues can be known by men; all that can be known of God is that he exists. They cannot, for this reason, be placed on the same scale.

37. Cf. *Ebr.* 112–13.

38. Holladay, *THEIOS ANER*, pp. 174–75.

39. *Ibid.*, pp. 175–76, esp. n. 331, marshals substantial evidence on this point.

40. Wolfson, *Philo*, I, 451.

41. Holladay, *THEIOS ANER*, p. 176.

42. Trans. Holladay, *ibid.*, p. 149.

43. See *supra*, p. 34.

44. Those, unlike Isaac and Moses, who are not born perfect must rely on a combination of these three elements. Philo, as is well known, assigns one element to each of the patriarchs. Cf. Dillon, *Middle Platonists*, pp. 152ff.

45. Wolfson, *Philo*, II, 47–48. Sandmel concurs in *Philo's Place*, p. 178, n. 347: "Not only is there in Philo no hint of the rabbinic view that prophecy ceased at the time of Ezra, but to the contrary, it is a continuing possession of the human race." Also see Drummond, *Philo Judaeus*, II, 282, and E. Fascher, *Prophētēs: Eine sprach- und religionsgeschichtliche Untersuchung* (Giessen, 1927), pp. 152–60.

46. Implicit in Winston, "Freedom and Determinism in Philo of Alexandria," pp. 68–69, n. 34, is a similar comparison.

47. Stählin in his article on *prokopē*, *TDNT* 6, 711, correctly draws our attention to *LA* iii.140–44 in which Philo notes "how a perfect man differs from one making gradual progress."

48. Cf. E. Fascher, "Abraham, *physiologos* und *philos theou*," *Mullus, Festschrift Theodor Klauser*, ed. A. Stuiber, A. Hermann (Münster, 1964), pp. 120–21.

49. Dey, *Intermediary World*, p. 40.

50. As the education of Abram indicates, the encyclical studies (also, significantly, called *mesē paideia*, *mesai epistēmai*, and *mesai technai*) are their métier. Kidd, "Stoic Intermediaries . . . ," p. 165, is correct to point out that "educative moral teaching [is] not directed towards the *sapiens* but to the *prokoptōn*."

51. Cf. Stählin, *prokopē*, *TDNT* 6, 709–11.

52. See *supra*, n. 31.

53. Wolfson, *Philo*, II, 89.

54. Borgen, *Bread*, p. 111, is correct when he says that Wolfson treats these problems "from the viewpoint of the philosophical question of cognition."

55. Cf. Sandmel, "Abraham's Knowledge of the Existence of God," *HTR* 44 (1951), 137–39, which speaks of a Bezalel class of men.

56. Also see *Som.* i.203–208.

57. Cf. *Mut.* 219.

58. This passage is cited by Guyot, *L'Infinité divine . . .*, p. 98, in the course of a discussion on ecstasy.

59. The main terms cited by Dey for this class of men are *phaulos*, *to tēs pros genesin zōēs genos*, and *anthrōpoi gēs* (*Intermediary World*, p. 40).

60. Cf. C. Siegfried, *Philo von Alexandria als Ausleger des alten Testaments* (Jena, 1875), pp. 249ff., in the section "Das Leben in der Sinnlichkeit."

61. I disagree with W. H. Wagner's contentions in "Philo and Paideia," *Cithara* 10 (1971),

54–56, that the *phaulos* represents the beginning stage of learning and that it is he who learns the encyclia. It is clear from the passages quoted here that the earth-born man learns nothing.

62. W. L. Knox, "Abraham and the Quest for God," *HTR* 28 (1935), 59.

63. A good example of this is *Heres* 45, quoted *supra*, pp. 48–49. Cf. *QG* iv.33: "Every foolish man is a narrow one, being constrained by love of money, love of pleasure, love of glory and similar things, which do not permit the mind to move in free space." Also see *Ebr.* 77–79.

64. Man has a "nature which apart from Divine bounty could obtain of itself no good thing" (*Opif.* 23). Cf. Alexandre, *De Congressu . . .* (ed.), pp. 75–76, and *supra*, pp. 38–39.

65. C. W. Larson, "Prayer of Petition in Philo," *JBL* 65 (1946), 201–202, states that "true humility and the desire for true virtue give assurance of God's favorable response." Even if this were so in Moses' case, it cannot be applied generally to ordinary men. There can be no assurance. Wolfson, *Philo,* I, 447–48, does not correct the problem.

66. *QG* iv.102: "One should not desire anything that is beyond one's capacity, for everything that has measure is praiseworthy."

67. Cf. *QG* iv.102: "Teaching should be more abundant for the intelligent man, and less for the foolish man."

68. The thoughts developed here are in accord with the fragment from the lost fourth book of *LA,* as it appears in Winston, "Freedom and Determinism in Philo of Alexandria," pp. 53–54: "Strictly speaking, the human mind does not choose the good through itself, but in accordance with the thoughtfulness of God, since He bestows the fairest things upon the worthy." Cf. *ibid.,* p. 66, n. 25. Also C. G. Montefiore, "Florilegium Philonis," *JQR* 7 (1895), 517, remarks that Philo "has to assume that men start with different endowments, and that these differences are predetermined by God."

69. See Diogenes Laertius, *Lives* vii. 91.

70. See, too, *Immut.* 144. J. Pascher, *Hē Basilikē Hodos: Der Königsweg zu Wiedergeburt und Vergöttung bei Philon von Alexandreia* (Paderborn, 1931), pp. 11–12, comments on this passage.

71. The Nimrod-type of man seems to appear in *Gig.* 20–21: "Even over the reprobate hovers often of a sudden the vision of the excellent, but to grasp it and keep it for their own they have not the strength. In a moment it is gone. . . ." Wolfson's analysis of this passage in *Philo,* I, 437–38, is unclear. The reprobate should not be vilified simply because of the briefness of his vision. Even a heaven-born man who is progressing satisfactorily may find that his vision of the excellent is fleeting. The Nimrod-type man is culpable because he has not developed the inward strength to grasp that which is shown to him.

For the juxtaposition of Nimrod and Abraham, see references in L. Ginzberg, *The Legends of the Jews* (Philadelphia, 1946) VII, 345. Also see G. Vermes, "The Life of Abraham (1)," *Scripture and Tradition in Judaism* (Leiden, 1961), pp. 67ff.

72. Winston's concept of relative free will, as set forth in "Freedom and Determinism in Philo of Alexandria" happily explains the apparent inconsistencies to be found in Philo. (The reader should also consult the background material presented by Winston in "Freedom and Determinism in Greek Philosophy and Jewish Hellenistic Wisdom," *SP* 2 [1973], 23–39.) Previous attempts to reconcile elements of Philo's thought, most notably Wolfson's in *Philo,* I, 442–46, are adequately treated by Winston. I would simply like to comment on Wolfson's belief that there is in Philo a "conception of divine aid or grace in the choice of good to those who have already by their general power of free will taken the initial steps towards the attainment of the good" (*ibid.,* p. 446). This is a useful formulation, but I should stress that it applies only to a limited group of men.

The extent to which Winston has advanced the study of this topic may be measured by a remark made by Montefiore at the end of the nineteenth century. In "Florilegium Philonis," 518, Montefiore plaintively comments that Philo "glides off" from some "deep problems" on the subject of free will. This is not to say that the concept of relative free will itself does not raise moral problems. Post-Enlightenment philosophers might reasonably ask: if Isaac is not "free" to do evil, then in what sense may his life be considered praiseworthy? The value of Winston's work is that he describes Philo's position so that it appears coherent within the original context.

73. Ultimately knowledge and virtue in Philo are one; the path to one is the same as the path to the other.

74. Far from viewing this alternative pejoratively, Philo himself often adopts this vantage point. (Cf. *supra*, pp. 34 and 55ff.) The two points of view described earlier correspond to that of the *sophos* and the *prokoptōn*.

The term "second-best voyage" (*deuteros plous*) appears in *Abr.* 123 and elsewhere in Philo as noted by Colson, *PLCL* V, 597 (on *Som.* i.44). For its use in Plato see, for instance, *Phaedo* 99D–102A.

75. The admonition not to be bold obviously applies to ordinary men only. A sage is only considered bold when he aspires to "inquire about essence or quality in God" (*Post.* 168–69). This boldness, recorded in the case of Moses (cf. *Fug.* 164–65 and *Mut.* 8–10), is of a different order and would not result in shipwreck. This is because the motivation of a sage in wanting to reach God, unlike that of the builders of the Tower of Babel (cf. *Som.* ii.285), is essentially good.

76. Cf. D. Winston, "Was Philo a Mystic?" SBL Seminar Papers (1978), pp. 165–69, esp. p. 165, n. 19. Also see *supra*, pp. 35–37.

77. Before considering the specific contribution of each patriarch to Philo's notion of man educated in virtue, we should take into account one complication. Each patriarch represents one of the three virtues mentioned above (cf. *supra*, n. 44)—instruction, nature, and practice. At the same time, Philo makes it clear that no patriarch is to be regarded solely in terms of the virtue he represents. Indeed, as Philo argues in *Abr.* 53, "each possesses the three qualities, but gets his name from that which chiefly predominates in him." In the following discussion of models for behavior, we should bear in mind the dual aspect of the patriarchs: first, as individuals whose particular strength is one primary character trait and, then, as figures who combine in themselves all virtues. Without denying the second aspect of patriarchal lives, I shall concentrate on the first.

78. Education by imitation had been an approved method from the time of Homer. For imitation in the archaic period, see Jaeger, *Paideia*, I, 32ff., and III, 62–65, as well as Marrou, *History*, pp. 34 and 286. Wolfson, *Philo*, II, 194–96, links imitation of God and native Jewish tradition.

79. The ultimate source of imitation is God himself. As Bréhier, *Idées*, p. 231, points out, God is depicted "as an excellent master, following the principles of Philonic pedagogy." Among God's more distinguished pupils are Moses and the patriarchs. Cf. *QG* iv.208: "He who uses God as teacher both profits and is competent to bring profit (to others)."

80. Also see *Praem.* 114–15: "To gaze continuously upon noble models (*paradeigmatōn*) imprints their likeness in souls which are not entirely hardened and stony. And therefore those who would imitate (*mimeisthai*) examples of good living so marvellous in their loveliness, are bidden not to despair of changing for the better." B. L. Mack comments on this passage in *"Imitatio Mosis,"SP* 1 (1972), 39.

81. Cf. Y. Amir, "Philo and the Bible," *SP* 2 (1973), 2–3.

82. Cf. S. W. Baron's assessment of history in Philo: "The element of history, so fundamental in the Jewish religion, evaporated here [in Philo] into the eternal, static categories of the philosophers. . . . In brief, to cite Siegfried's apt characterization, 'the history of his people, though literally believed to be true, became in his treatment essentially a didactic and symbolic poem.'" (*A Social and Religious History of the Jews*, I, 205–6. Baron's quotation of Siegfried is from the latter's *Philo von Alexandria als Ausleger . . .*, p. 159.)

Philo sums up his own view regarding "events" in the Bible in this way: "The inquiry of the theologian is about characters and types and virtues, and not about persons who were created and born" (*QG* iv.137). Also see *Cong.* 180 and *Ebr.* 144.

83. On these criteria, the corpus of classical Greek historians, playwrights, and poets contains nothing of value. Philo would have considered their work as providing only "unimproving entertainment." On no level does it provide man with truths. Cf. Philo's reference to those lawgivers

who, "dressing up their ideas in much irrelevant and cumbersome matter, have befogged the masses and hidden the truth under their fictions" (*Opif.* 1).

84. The translation here is that of Mack, *"Imitatio Mosis,"* p. 27. See Mack's discussion of the phrase *eis meson proagagōn, ibid.,* p. 42, n. 3.

85. Cf. *ibid.,* p. 37: "Grasped as a whole and viewed from its *telos* its course becomes a graphic pattern to be looked at all at one time. In the case of Moses' *bios* the *telos* is cosmic ascent, so corresponding to the grand cosmic way of Philo's allegory, and it is transformation via vision into 'a single unity,' 'a mind pure as the sunlight' [*Mos.* ii.288], thus reflecting the aspect of (ar)rest and completion."

86. Cf. Seneca's view that human beings do not ordinarily become *sophoi* in *Epistles* 42.1 and 95.36. This does not mean that the one *sophos* who is born in five hundred years should not be emulated.

87. Cf. Marcus, "Outline of Philo's System of Education," p. 229.

88. Goodenough, *Light,* p. 241.

89. I do not agree with Colson, "Philo on Education," p. 161, that the speed with which Moses outgrew his teachers shows that Philo did not appreciate teachers in general. Surely Moses' is a unique case of learning. Furthermore, imitation, which is central to Philo's system of education, requires teachers.

90. Cf. *Det.* 124, *Abr.* 194; and Goodenough, *Light,* pp. 154-55.

91. H. Leisegang, *Der heilige Geist* (Leipzig, 1919), pp. 149-50.

92. E.g., *Abr.* 50-54. In identifying each of the patriarchs with one element in the educational triad of learning (*mathēsis* = Abraham), nature (*physis* = Isaac), and practice (*askēsis* = Jacob), Philo seems to have put the triad to a new use. Note too that after identifying the patriarchs in this way, Philo also blurs the distinctions, as in *QG* iv.144. See Wolfson, *Philo,* II, 196-98; Siegfried, *Philo von Alexandria als Ausleger . . .*, pp. 256f.; Montefiore, "Florilegium Philonis," p. 517; Sandmel, *Philo's Place,* pp. 142-43, esp. n. 207; Dillon, *Middle Platonists,* pp. 152-53; Tiede, *Charismatic Figure,* pp. 110-11; and Colson, "Philo on Education," p. 160, esp. n. 2. Although Jaeger does not relate his discussion to Philo, the reader is referred to his *Paideia,* I, 305-6 and 312-13. Also see Harry Caplan, *Cicero: Ad C. Herennium* (London, 1964), p. 7, n. c. Cf. *supra,* nn. 44 and 77.

93. Hengel, *Judaism and Hellenism,* I, 91-92 with nn. 264-66 (in II, 62-63); and I, 302. Also see Sandmel, *Philo's Place,* pp. 38-59.

94. G. Mayer, "Aspekte des Abrahambildes in der hellenistisch-jüdischen Literatur," *Evangelische Theologie* 32 (1972), 118-27. For a fuller discussion of Abraham as a missionary see B. E. Schein, "Our Father, Abraham," pp. 40-51. Cf. L. H. Feldman, "Abraham the Greek Philosopher in Josephus," *Transactions and Proceedings of the American Philological Association* 99 (1968), 143-56. While noting differences in their respective treatments, Feldman points out that both Philo and Josephus try to make Abraham appeal to Greek readers. Also see B. Z. Wacholder, "Pseudo-Eupolemos' Two Greek Fragments on the Life of Abraham," *HUCA* 34 (1963), 83-113; and Knox, "Abraham and the Quest for God," p. 59.

95. D. M. Hay, "Philo's Treatise on the Logos-Cutter," *SP* 2 (1973), 12.

96. Cf. Sandmel, *Philo's Place,* p. 198, n. 407: "There are several passages in which Philo makes a personal application of the scriptural lesson he has inferred about Abraham. He urges his own soul to imitate Abraham's migration, *Heres* 69ff. Philo, too, wanted to beget out of virtue, Sarah, *Cong.* 6, cf. *Mut.* 255ff. The mating with the encyclia is Philo's experience also, *Cong.* 88. The *ecstasis* of Abraham, *Heres* 68, is paralleled by Philo's own *ecstasis, Mig.* 34-35."

CHAPTER 4

1. This pre-Socratic fragment was quoted in the introduction to the present work at n. 36. For further discussion of this important maxim, see Alexandre, *De Congressu . . .* (ed.), pp. 61ff.; Col-

son, "Philo on Education," p. 154; de Rijk, *"Enkyklios paideia,"* pp. 82ff.; Wolfson, *Philo,* I, 145–46; Borgen, *Bread,* p. 108, esp. n. 1; and H. Chadwick, "St. Paul and Philo of Alexandria," *Bulletin of the John Rylands Library* 48, no. 2 (1966), 299.

2. The main problem raised by this analogy is the precise meaning of the term "philosophy." We may start with the analogy as it appears to be given. That is, the maidservants: Penelope :: Hagar : Sarah :: encyclical studies : philosophy. The precise content of the final term has raised the most debate. In a private conversation, Professor S. Daniel suggested to me that "philosophy" here means "Torah" and that "pagan philosophy" (for purposes of argument let us say this would refer to Plato) would have to be relegated to the encyclia. By this reasoning the analogy would become—Hagar : Sarah :: encyclical studies *and* pagan philosophy : Torah. In support of this argument, it was pointed out that "pagan philosophy" could be subsumed under the encyclical studies of rhetoric and dialectic. A. M. Malingrey, *Philosophia; étude d'un groupe de mots dans la littérature grecque, des Présocratiques au IV siècle après J.-C.* (Paris, 1961), pp. 77–91, argues along the same lines, insisting that the *cosmos* is the substance of philosophy for Philo.

Both the reader mentioned above and Malingrey err in thinking that for Philo the cosmos itself is the substance of philosophy. Although it is true that in the *Timaeus* 47 and in *Opif.* 54–56, philosophy arises out of number which in turn arises out of contemplation of the cosmos, a process of abstraction clearly has taken place. Philosophy still occupies the highest immaterial segment of the Divided Line in Plato, as it would in Philo. We should also consider several other points. In Philo, classical philosophy (mainly as represented by Plato) and Torah tend to merge. As long as one can ask, "What is Plato but the Attic Moses?" on some level it is very difficult to distinguish between them. Philo *thought* of Creation in Platonic terms; he differed from Plato only where he had to. But let us suppose for a moment that we could distinguish Philo's philosophical commitments from his loyalty to the Torah. Instead of redefining philosophy by placing it among the encyclia, we may simply add two other terms to the ratio given above. The ratio would then be extended to read, as *Cong.* 79 suggests. . . . encyclical studies : philosophy :: philosophy : wisdom. Here wisdom (or *sophia*) is Torah; it is beyond pagan philosophy. But both Torah and pagan philosophy are part of the immaterial world. On this point see Winston's remarks in Colloquy 15, p. 19, and in "Was Philo a Mystic?" p. 164; Henrichs, "Philosophy, the Handmaiden . . .," pp. 437–45; and Amir, "Philo and the Bible," p. 5.

3. The opposite images which Philo associates with philosophy are, respectively: the "chamber doors" of a house and the "inner part" of cities (*Cong.* 10), royalty, the solid and costly foods of adults, the Hebrew race, and the "native born, indigenous, citizens in the truest sense" (*ibid.,* 22).

4. Cf. *Prob.* 160.

5. This analogy reappears in *QG* iv.244. We should recall here the general inferiority of women as discussed *supra,* p. 28.

6. For analogies not listed here see Colson's "Introduction," *PLCL* I, xvi–xvii. Alexandre, *De Congressu* . . . (ed.), pp. 69–71 discusses some of the images (other than Hagar) used by Philo in portraying the encyclia.

7. Drummond, *Philo Judaeus,* I, 262. The same idea may be found in Billings, *The Platonism of Philo Judaeus,* p. 86; Colson, *PLCL* I, xvii; E. Zeller, *Die Philosophie der Griechen* (Leipzig, 1903), III, Pt. II, 457; Wolfson, *Philo,* I, 145–46; J. Bowen, *A History of Western Education,* I, 231–34. Cf. Völker, *Fortschritt* . . ., pp. 172–75 and Drazin, *The History of Jewish Education* . . ., pp. 92–93.

8. Leisegang, *Geist,* p. 62.

9. Boughton, "The Idea of Progress in Philo Judaeus," p. 217, notes that "when a man has thus risen he becomes a lover of God and may look back upon the things of the body to observe how good God has been to provide a world in which even the inferior and inanimate things have their appropriate uses."

10. Sandmel, *Philo's Place,* p. 155, remarks that "Abraham understands, as other minds do not, that the encyclia are only preparatory stages. . . ."

11. Cf. *supra,* p. 4, n. 23.

12. Philo gives one overview of the process in *Mig.* 194–95.

13. Hans Lewy gives a summary of these stages in *Philosophical Writings: Philo* (Oxford, 1946), p. 19. Lewy mentions that skepticism plays a key role, but he does not say how it fits into the ascent.

14. At this point in the progressive man's career he is simply learning at first hand what Philo depicted as the nature of encyclical studies; cf. *supra*, pp. 35–37.

15. Cf. *Som.* i.53–54, which is similar in substance and purpose. Also see R. M. Grant, "Irenaeus and Hellenistic Culture," *HTR* 42 (1949), 41f., and the same author's *Miracle and Natural Law* (Amsterdam, 1952), pp. 78–81. For further references to and discussion of Philo's use of doxographical materials, see *PLCL* V, 594–95.

16. It is no wonder that in his depiction of the Essenes Philo has them abandon the physical part of philosophy "as beyond the grasp of human nature" (*Prob.* 80).

17. The tropes do not appear elsewhere until Sextus Empiricus and Diogenes Laertius take them up. See Colson's notes in *PLCL* III, 505–508; *Middle Platonists*, p. 144; Long, *Hellenistic Philosophy*, pp. 75f., esp. n. 1, p. 75; and R. G. Hamerton-Kelly, "Sources and Traditions in Philo Judaeus," *SP* 1, 6. Notes 20–23 of the latter work refer to H. von Arnim, "Quellenstudien zu Philo von Alexandria" (Berlin, 1888), *q.v.* for full references.

18. Philo's views here seem to have provoked at least one scholar to adopt a rather extreme view of Philo on sense perception. See the remarks of M. Freudenthal, *Die Erkenntnislehre Philos von Alexandria* (Berlin, 1891), p. 19: "There is no 'objective' reality, for there are no objects; everything is illusion. There is no science (*Wissenschaft*), for there is no knowledge (*Wissen*); everything is opinion. We perceive that the corporeal world is deceptive from its instability. Nothing is permanent and constant in it. Everything flows in eternal flux." Cf. U. Früchtel, *Die kosmologischen Vorstellungen . . .*, pp. 160ff.

19. *PLCL* III, 314, n. *a*.

20. In *Ebr.* 33–34 Philo refers to "rules laid down by human ordinance, rules which have been made in different cities and countries and nations by those who first embraced the apparent in preference to the true." Philo explicitly places these rules on an encyclical level.

21. Goodenough discusses this issue in *The Politics of Philo Judaeus,* p. 81: "In a long discussion of the unreliability of our perceptions Philo's chief illustration of human fallibility is the extreme divergence of civil laws in the various parts of the world. . . . In this passage Philo's only conclusion is that we must suspend judgment upon specific definitions of the good, since even philosophers are in disagreement upon every essential point. . . . Philo is consistently dualistic in his view of human nature and of the two laws to which man is subject. On the one hand, by virtue of his divine mind, man is naturally a citizen of the Cosmopolis, subject to the divine laws of Nature. As a man of material nature he is just as naturally given to producing civil law, and subject to its authority. But while the two laws are both in a sense the product of Nature, there is usually no lineal connection, much as there should be, between civil law as it is and natural law. Our civic law is actually a travesty rather than a reflection of Nature."

22. Cf. *Conf.* 114–15.

23. Not every problem raised by Philo's use of skepticism can be resolved in this way. In certain contexts skepticism has a different function. For instance, Philo may use it to denigrate a particular view of the world with which he is not in sympathy. Cf. A. Weische, *Cicero und die neue Akademie* (Münster, 1961), pp. 99–100, and Michel, "Quelques aspects . . .," p. 97. In agreeing with Weische, Michel says that Philo's skepticism is only directed against opinions of the world in which Joseph acts, not against knowledge itself or the existence of the intelligible world.

24. Those who maintain juxtaposed opinions are explicitly identified with "sophists" in *Heres* 246–48. Sophistic strife and skepticism disappear only with the introduction of a sage, here called a "man-midwife."

25. Drummond, *Philo Judaeus,* I, 325–27, offers us a case of Philo's initial skepticism being replaced by a well-founded belief in one particular view. It is no accident that that view corresponds to Scripture.

26. Cf. Jonas, *Gnosis,* pp. 103f.

27. Also see *Fug.* 132–36 in which sense perception virtually yields speechlessness.

28. Wolfson, *Philo*, II, 7; cf. *supra*, p. 35, n. 59.

29. Philo also employs imagery to depict the same experience. For his use of darkness prior to the light of divine knowledge, see Rist, *Eros and Psyche: Studies in Plato, Plotinus, and Origen* (Toronto, 1964), p. 189.

30. In *Opif.* 69–71, for an example, Philo sketches the spiritual development of man from the encyclia "to the topmost arch of things perceptible to mind." But lost in rapture over the transformation, he does not mention that skepticism is a stage in the mind's movement "beyond the confines of all substance discernible by sense."

31. For Abraham and astral speculation in Jewish tradition, see Ginzberg, *The Legends of the Jews*, V, 175, n. 19, and esp. p. 227, n. 108. Also see Sandmel, *Philo's Place*, pp. 55, 60–62, 79–80, and 92.

32. For a study of differences between the Greek understanding of the Delphic maxim and Philo's, see P. Courcelle, "Philon d'Alexandrie et le précepte delphique," *Philomathes: Studies and Essays in the Humanities in Memory of Philip Merlan* (ed. R. B. Palmer and R. Hamerton-Kelly; The Hague, 1971), 245–50. Also see, J.-G. Kahn, "'Connais-toi toi même' à la manière de Philon," *Revue d'histoire et de philosophie religieuses* 53 (1973), 293–307. While I do not think that Philo promoted the acquisition of knowledge of the material world *solely* for the purpose of the negations which follow, Kahn's article is a contribution to several aspects of Philo's thought touched upon in this chapter.

33. Cf. Jonas, *Gnosis*, pp. 106f.

34. Cf. *Mig.* 134.

35. See the initial characterization of this route *supra*, pp. 55–58.

36. See *Mut.* 220: "Moses taught us to make our acknowledgements of thanks according to the power of our hands (Num. vi.21), the man of sagacity dedicating his good sense and prudence, the master of words consecrating all the excellences of speech in praises to the Existent in poem or prose, and from others offerings after their kind, natural philosophy, ethical philosophy, the lore of the arts and sciences (*ta theōrēmata tōn technōn kai epistēmōn*) from the several students of the same."

37. To my knowledge, no one has discussed the encyclia from the ordinary man's point of view. Only Alexandre, *De Congressu . . .* (ed.), pp. 78–79, has hinted that Philo's treatment of the subject might be more complex than it appears at first sight: "Philo . . . proceeds by complementary affirmations: the liberal arts prepare for perfection, they are inferior to it. The double side of the images corresponds to this. The *enkyklios paideia* is at the same time maid-servant and slave, residence but the residence of a stranger, nourishment but milky nourishment. The accent sometimes rests on the positive aspect, sometimes on the relative aspect of *paideia*. It is necessary to take account of these tensions." Alexandre errs here only in understating the case, for the "positive aspect" is more thoroughly grounded than she indicates. Alexandre (*ibid.*, p. 79, n. 1) certainly is correct to take issue with Bréhier, *Idées*, p. 284, who maintains that it is in a "spirit of curiosity without any serious foundation, that Philo treats the encyclicals and the sciences which are connected to them." Bréhier (*ibid.*, p. 282) is also mistaken in the inferences he draws from the fact that Philo gives only fragmentary information about the actual disciplines.

38. In the previous section of this chapter, I noted that the sage ultimately views the material world in a negative light. The ordinary man, the subject of our present inquiries, has a positive orientation toward the material world; cf. *supra*, p. 34.

39. See *supra*, pp. 35–36.

40. What is particularly interesting about this passage is that while Philo refers to Bezalel, who is mentioned in Ex. 31.2, he does not consider the next Biblical verse in any detail. Ex. 31.3, in the LXX, says that Bezalel is filled "with a divine spirit of wisdom, and understanding, and knowledge" (*pneuma theion sophias kai syneseōs kai epistēmēs*). I suspect that Philo did not wax eloquent on this verse because, if it would refer to anyone in Philonic terms, it would be to a sage rather than

to a progressive man like Bezalel. Although an argument from silence is dangerous, the fact that Philo does not elaborate on Ex. 31.3 would seem to indicate that he was consciously trying to preserve his typology of men.

41. For a brief history of this argument, see M. L. Clarke, *Paley: Evidences for the Man* (London, 1974), pp. 89–90. Clarke notes that the argument "is found in all its essentials" in Xenophon, *Memorabilia* i.4.5–7 and in Cicero, *De Natura Deorum*. In the latter work, a speaker asks this rhetorical question: "When we gaze upward to the sky and contemplate the heavenly bodies, what can be so obvious and so manifest as that there must exist some power possessing transcendent intelligence by whom these things are ruled?" (ii.4). Cicero finds traces of these ideas among the pre-Socratics: "Anaxagoras . . . was the first thinker to hold that the orderly disposition of the universe is designed and perfected by the rational power of an infinite mind" (i.26). (The passages quoted here are from the *LCL* edition, trans. H. Rackham.) To my mind Philo's emphasis is somewhat different from that of Cicero. For Philo the transcendent intelligence not only designs and rules the universe, but also *creates* it. Wolfson, *Philo,* II, 75–78, discusses this argument as it appears in Philo, classical authors, and rabbinic sources (cf. esp. *ibid.,* II, 77, n. 22). Also see Drummond, *Philo Judaeus,* II, 2–4.

42. The passage parallel to this in Cicero is *De Natura Deorum* ii.15.

43. E.g., the numerical laws governing music, if understood in sufficient depth, could precede divine knowledge.

44. Cf. *Spec.* i.49–50.

45. The return to the encyclia is reminiscent of the return to the Cave by those who have seen the Good in Plato's *Republic* vii.516–19.

46. For instance, Philo is aware that it is difficult to give a scientific account of the Milky Way; nevertheless "students of natural phenomena must not shrink from the quest" (*Provid.* ii.51). Philo makes a general statement on the quest in *LA* iii.47: "The mere seeking by itself is sufficient to make us partakers of good things, for it always is the case that endeavours after noble things, even if they fail to attain their object, gladden in their very course those who make them." Also see *Spec.* i.36–40.

47. *The Wisdom of the Desert: Sayings from the Desert Fathers of the Fourth Century* (trans. T. Merton; New York, 1960), p. 62, no. 103.

CONCLUSION

1. Cf. *Republic* vii.522–539. Also see R. L. Nettleship, *Lectures on the Republic of Plato* (London, 1937), p. 269, and J. E. Raven, *Plato's Thought in the Making* (Cambridge, 1965), pp. 178ff.

2. Holladay, *THEIOS ANER,* pp. 110f.

3. R. P. McKeon, "The Liberating and Humanizing Arts in Education," *Humanistic Education and Western Civilization,* ed. A. A. Cohen (New York, 1964), pp. 163–64.

4. This is by no means a universally accepted position. Cf. Bréhier, *Idées,* pp. 294–95, who claims that Philo "unceasingly seems to fear the effects of Hellenic education, this culture of intellect for its own sake without practical result, this exercise of talent which does not make men better. . . ." Needless to say, one could take issue both with Bréhier's view of Philo's attitude and his concept of Hellenic education itself.

5. Naturally I am assuming that Philo evolved these ideas before the Letter of Claudius to the Alexandrians (41 C.E.) ordered the Jews not to intrude themselves in Greek institutions (*CPJ,* II, No. 153, ll.92–95).

6. On the misuses of education see *supra,* pp. 44ff.

7. Cf. *Mos.* ii.211 and my remarks *supra,* p. 32.

8. There are, of course, other obvious examples of line-drawing. For instance, I believe that Philo entered the Greek gymnasium despite the fact that gymnasia had busts of deities (cf. *supra,*

pp. 31–32). Yet Philo was outraged when the statue of a man, with chariot and four horses, was taken from the gymnasium to the Jews' house of worship where it was dedicated to the deified Gaius (*Legat.* 136). Tributes to the emperors were allowed in the meeting-houses (*Legat.* 133), but there Philo drew the line.

9. Cf. Shroyer, "Alexandrian Jewish Literalists," 261ff.

10. Certainly the independence of the community is already clear in the Letter of Aristeas. Cf. A. Momigliano, *Alien Wisdom: The Limits of Hellenization* (Cambridge, 1975), p. 116.

11. We may infer that Jews of Philo's persuasion were observant, at least in their own eyes. This is clear from Philo's denunciation of the extreme allegorists, who are depicted as having abandoned the letter of the law.

12. *CPJ*, I, 78. Greeks and Jews were natural rivals for the "affections" of Rome. When Rome favored the Jews, as she did in granting the Jews a council of elders (*gerousia*), the Greeks were angered; cf. A. Segré, "The Status of the Jews in Ptolemaic and Roman Egypt," *Jewish Social Studies* 6 (1944), 389; H. I. Bell, "Anti-Semitism in Alexandria," *Journal of Roman Studies* 31 (1941), 4; and J. L. Daniel, "Anti-Semitism in the Hellenistic-Roman Period," *JBL* 98 (1979), 45–65.

A Select Bibliography

BIBLIOGRAPHICAL SOURCES

Marcus, Ralph. "Recent Literature on Philo (1924–1934)," *Jewish Studies in Memory of George A. Kohut,* New York, 1935. Pp. 463–91.

Goodhart, Howard L. and Erwin R. Goodenough. *General Bibliography of Philo.* Published in Goodenough's *The Politics of Philo Judaeus.* New Haven, 1938.

Feldman, Louis. *Studies in Judaica: Scholarship on Philo and Josephus (1937–1962).* New York, n.d.

Hilgert, Earle. "A Bibliography of Philo Studies, 1963–1970," *SP* 1, 57–71. (In each succeeding volume of *SP,* Hilgert has contributed an updated bibliography. At present bibliographies are available up to and including *SP* 5.)

SECONDARY SOURCES, BOOKS

Alexandre, Monique. *De congressu eruditionis gratia.* "Les oeuvres de Philon d'Alexandrie," Vol. 16. Paris, 1967.

Amand, David. *Fatalisme et liberté dans l'antiquité grecque.* Louvain, 1945.

Baer, Richard A., Jr. *Philo's Use of the Categories Male and Female.* Leiden, 1970.

Baron, Salo Wittmayer. *A Social and Religious History of the Jews.* Vol. I–II: *Ancient Times.* 2nd ed. rev. Philadelphia, 1952.

Belkin, Samuel. *Philo and the Oral Law.* Cambridge, 1940.

Bieler, Ludwig. *THEIOS ANER: Das Bild des "göttlichen Menschen" in Spätantike und Frühchristentum.* 2 vols. Wien, 1935.

Billings, Thomas H. *The Platonism of Philo Judaeus.* Chicago, 1919.

Borgen, Peder. *Bread from Heaven.* Leiden, 1965.

Boughton, Jesse Scott. "The Idea of Progress in Philo Judaeus." Unpublished diss., Faculty of Philosophy, Columbia University, 1932.

Bowen, James. *A History of Western Education.* 2 vols. New York, 1972.

Box, Herbert. *Philonis Alexandrini: In Flaccum.* London, 1939.

Braun, Martin. *History and Romance in Graeco-Oriental Literature.* Oxford, 1938.

Bréhier, Émile. *Les idées philosophiques et religieuses de Philon d'Alexandrie.* Paris, 1908.

Clarke, M. L. *Higher Education in the Ancient World.* London, 1971.

Cumont, Franz. *Astrology and Religion among the Greeks and Romans.* American Lectures on the History of Religions, Series of 1911–1912. New York, 1912.

Daniélou, Jean. *Philon d'Alexandrie.* Paris, 1958.

Dey, Lala Kalyan Kumar. *The Intermediary World and Patterns of Perfection in Philo and Hebrews.* Society of Biblical Literature Dissertation Series, No. 25. Missoula, 1975.

Dillon, John. *The Middle Platonists: A Study of Platonism 80 B.C. to A.D. 220.* London, 1977.

Drazin, Nathan. *The History of Jewish Education from 515 B.C.E. to 220 C.E.* Johns Hopkins University Studies in Education, 29. Baltimore, 1940.

Drummond, James. *Philo Judaeus; or, the Jewish-Alexandrian Philosophy in Its Development and Completion.* 2 vols. London, 1888.

Ebner, E. *Elementary Education in Ancient Israel during the Tanaitic Period (10–220 C.E.).* New York, 1956.

Fascher, E. *Prophētēs: Eine sprach- und religionsgeschichtliche Untersuchung.* Giessen, 1927.
Fischel, Henry A. *Essays in Greco-Roman and Related Talmudic Literature.* New York, 1977.
———. *Rabbinic Literature and Greco-Roman Philosophy.* Leiden, 1973.
Fraser, P. M. *Ptolemaic Alexandria.* 3 vols. Oxford, 1972.
Freudenthal, Max. *Die Erkenntnislehre Philos von Alexandria.* Berlin, 1891.
Früchtel, Ursula. *Die kosmologischen Vorstellungen bei Philo von Alexandrien.* Leiden, 1968.
Fuchs, Leo. *Die Juden Aegyptens in ptolemäischer und römischer Zeit.* Wien, 1924.
Ginzberg, Louis. *The Legends of the Jews,* trans. Henrietta Szold. 7 vols. Philadelphia, 1925–38.
Goodenough, Erwin R. *By Light, Light: The Mystic Gospel of Hellenistic Judaism.* New Haven, 1935.
———. *An Introduction to Philo Judaeus.* 2nd ed. rev. Oxford, 1962.
———. *Jewish Symbols in the Greco-Roman Period.* 13 vols. New York, 1953–68.
———. *The Jurisprudence of the Jewish Courts in Egypt.* New Haven, 1929.
———. *The Politics of Philo Judaeus.* New Haven, 1938.
Grant, Robert M. *Augustus to Constantine.* London, 1971.
———. *Miracle and Natural Law.* Amsterdam, 1952.
Guyot, Henri. *L'Infinité divine depuis Philon le Juif jusqu'à Plotin.* Paris, 1906.
Heinemann, Isaak. *Philons griechische und jüdische Bildung.* Breslau, 1932.
Hengel, Martin. *Judaism and Hellenism: Studies in Their Encounter in Palestine during the Early Hellenistic Period,* trans. from 2nd rev. ed. by J. Bowden. 2 vols. London, 1974.
Herriot, Édouard. *Philon le Juif: essai sur l'école juive d'alexandrie.* Paris, 1898.
Holladay, Carl R. *THEIOS ANER in Hellenistic Judaism: A Critique of the Use of This Category in New Testament Christology.* Society of Biblical Literature Dissertation Series, No. 40. Missoula, 1977.
Jaeger, Werner. *Paideia: The Ideals of Greek Culture,* trans. Gilbert Highet. 3 vols. Oxford, 1939–45.
Jentsch, Werner. *Urchristliches Erziehungsdenken: Die Paideia Kyriu im Rahmen der hellenistisch-jüdischen Umwelt.* Gütersloh, 1951.
Jonas, Hans. *Gnosis und spätantiker Geist.* Pt. II, 1. 2nd ed. rev. Göttingen, 1966.
Jones, A. H. M. *The Cities of the Eastern Roman Provinces.* Oxford, 1971.
Keferstein, Friedrich. *Philo's Lehre von den göttlichen Mittelwesen.* Leipzig, 1846.
Kühnert, Friedmar. *Allgemeinbildung und Fachbildung in der Antike.* Deutsche Akademie der Wissenschaften, vol. 30. Berlin, 1961.
Leisegang, Hans. *Der heilige Geist.* Leipzig, 1919.
Lewy, Hans (ed.). *Philosophical Writings: Philo.* Oxford, 1946.
Lieberman, Saul. *Greek in Jewish Palestine.* New York, 1965.
———. *Hellenism in Jewish Palestine.* 2nd ed. New York, 1962.
Lodge, R. C. *Plato's Theory of Education.* London, 1947.
Long, A. A. *Hellenistic Philosophy: Stoics, Epicureans, Sceptics.* London, 1974.
Marrou, H. I. *A History of Education in Antiquity,* trans. George Lamb for the New American Library. New York, 1964.
———. *Saint Augustin et la fin de la culture antique.* Paris, 1938.
Meeks, Wayne A. *The Prophet-King: Moses Traditions and the Johannine Christology.* Leiden, 1967.
Momigliano, Arnaldo. *Alien Wisdom: The Limits of Hellenization.* Cambridge, 1975.
Morris, Nathan. *The Jewish School.* London, 1937.
Nettleship, Richard L. *Lectures on the Republic of Plato.* London, 1937.
Nilsson, M. P. *Die hellenistische Schule.* München, 1955.
Pascher, J. *Hē Basilikē Hodos: Der Königsweg zu Wiedergeburt und Vergöttung bei Philon von Alexandreia.* Paderborn, 1931.
Rist, J. M. *Eros and Psyche: Studies in Plato, Plotinus, and Origen.* Toronto, 1964.
———. *Stoic Philosophy.* Cambridge, 1969.
Sandmel, Samuel. *Philo of Alexandria: An Introduction.* New York, 1979.
———. *Philo's Place in Judaism: A Study of Conceptions of Abraham in Jewish Literature,* augmented ed. New York, 1971.

Schein, Bruce Edward. "Our Father Abraham." Unpublished diss., Yale University, 1972.

Siegfried, Carl. *Philo von Alexandria als Ausleger des alten Testaments.* Jena, 1875.

Smallwood, E. Mary. *Philonis Alexandrini: Legatio ad Gaium.* Leiden, 1961.

Smith, Robert W. *The Art of Rhetoric in Alexandria: Its Theory and Practice in the Ancient World.* The Hague, 1974.

Staehle, Karl. *Die Zahlenmystik bei Philon von Alexandreia.* Leipzig, 1931.

Stern, Menachem. *Greek and Latin Authors on Jews and Judaism: From Herodotus to Plutarch.* Jerusalem, 1976.

Tcherikover, Victor A. *Hellenistic Civilization and the Jews,* trans. S. Applebaum. Philadelphia, 1959.

Thorndike, Lynn. *A History of Magic and Experimental Science.* Vol. I. New York, 1923.

Tiede, David L. *The Charismatic Figure as Miracle Worker.* Society of Biblical Literature Dissertation Series, No. 1. Missoula, 1972.

Tsekourakis, Damianos. *Studies in the Terminology of Early Stoic Ethics. Hermes: Zeitschrift für klassische Philologie, Heft* 32. Wiesbaden, 1974.

Völker, Walther. *Fortschritt und Vollendung bei Philo von Alexandrien. Texte und Untersuchungen zur Geschichte der altchristlichen Literatur.* Vol. 49, Pt. 1. Leipzig, 1938.

Wacholder, Ben Zion. *Eupolemus: A Study of Judaeo-Greek Literature.* Monographs of the Hebrew Union College, 3. Cincinnati, 1974.

Weische, Alfons. *Cicero und die neue Akademie.* Münster, 1961.

Williamson, R. *Philo and the Epistle to the Hebrews.* Leiden, 1970.

Wolfson, Harry Austryn. *Philo: Foundations of Religious Philosophy in Judaism, Christianity, and Islam.* 2 vols. 4th printing, rev. Cambridge, 1968.

SECONDARY SOURCES, ARTICLES

Alexandre, Monique. "La culture profane chez Philon," *PAL,* 105–30.

Amir, Yehoshua. "Philo and the Bible," *SP* 2 (1973), 1–8.

Argyle, A. W. "The Ancient University of Alexandria," *Classical Journal* 69 (1974), 348–50.

Baumgarten, H. "Vitam brevem esse, longam artem," *Gymnasium* 77 (1970), 299–323.

Bell, H. I. "Anti-Semitism in Alexandria," *Journal of Roman Studies* 31 (1941), 1–18.

Boyancé, P. "Études philoniennes," *Revue des études grecques* 76 (1963), 82–95.

Brady, Thomas A. "The Gymnasium in Ptolemaic Egypt," *University of Missouri Studies,* Vol. 11, No. 3 (1936), 9–20.

Chadwick, Henry. "Philo and the Beginnings of Christian Thought," *The Cambridge History of Later Greek and Early Medieval Philosophy,* ed. A. H. Armstrong. Cambridge, 1967. Pp. 137–57.

———. "St. Paul and Philo of Alexandria," *Bulletin of the John Rylands Library,* Vol. 48, No. 2 (1966), 286–307.

Cohen, Shaye. "The Hellenization of Rabbinic Judaism: The State of the Question and Some Suggestions for Further Research" (unpublished paper written for the Consultation on Hellenistic Judaism, Society of Biblical Literature, 1977).

Colson, F. H. "Philo on Education," *JTS* 18 (1916–17), 151–62.

———. "Philo's Quotations from the Old Testament," *JTS* 41 (1940), 237–51.

Conley, T. *"General Education" in Philo of Alexandria,* Center for Hermeneutical Studies in Hellenistic and Modern Culture, No. 15. Berkeley, 1975.

Courcelle, P. "Philon d'Alexandrie et le précepte delphique," *Philomathes: Studies and Essays in the Humanities in Memory of Philip Merlan,* ed. R. B. Palmer and R. Hamerton-Kelly. The Hague, 1971. Pp. 245–50.

Davidson, Thomas. "The Seven Liberal Arts," *Educational Review* 2 (1891), 467–73.

Dillon, J., and A. Terian. "Philo and the Stoic Doctrine of *Eupatheiai,*" *SP* 4 (1976–77), 17–24.

Fascher, E. "Abraham, *physiologos* und *philos theou,*" *Mullus, Festschrift Theodor Klauser,* ed. A. Stuiber, A. Hermann. Münster, 1964. Pp. 111–24.

Feldman, Louis H. "Abraham the Greek Philosopher in Josephus," *Transactions and Proceedings of the American Philological Association* 99 (1968), 143–56.

———. "Hengel's *Judaism and Hellenism* in Retrospect," *JBL* 96 (1977), 371–82.

———. "The Orthodoxy of the Jews in Hellenistic Egypt," *Jewish Social Studies* 22 (1960), 215–37.

Foster, S. Stephen. "A Note on the 'Note' of J. Schwarz," *SP* 4 (1976–77), 25–32.

Goodenough, Erwin R. "Literal Mystery in Hellenistic Judaism," *Quantulacumque,* eds. R. P. Casey, S. Lake and A. K. Lake. London, 1937. Pp. 227–41.

Grant, Robert M. "Irenaeus and Hellenistic Culture," *HTR* 42 (1949), 41–51.

Hallewy, E. E. "Concerning the Ban on Greek Wisdom" (Hebrew), *Tarbiz* 41 (1972), 269–74.

Hamerton-Kelly, R. G. "Sources and Traditions in Philo Judaeus," *SP* 1 (1972), 3–26.

Hay, D. M. "Philo's Treatise on the Logos-Cutter," *SP* 2 (1973), 9–22.

Henrichs, A. "Philosophy, the Handmaiden of Theology," *Greek, Roman, and Byzantine Studies* 9 (1968), 437–50.

Kahn, J.-G. "'Connais-toi toi-même' à la manière de Philon," *Revue d'histoire et de philosophie religieuses* 53 (1973), 293–307.

Kidd, I. G. "Stoic Intermediaries and the End for Man," *Problems in Stoicism,* ed. A. A. Long. London, 1971. Pp. 150–72.

Knox, W. L. "Abraham and the Quest for God," *HTR* 28 (1935), 55–60.

Koller, Hermann. *"Enkyklios Paideia," Glotta* 34 (1955), 174–89.

Laroche, E. "Les noms grecs de l'astronomie," *Revue de Philologie* 20 (1946), 118–23.

Larson, Curtis W. "Prayer of Petition in Philo," *JBL* 65 (1946), 185–203.

Lieberman, Saul. "How Much Greek in Jewish Palestine?" *Texts and Studies.* New York, 1974. Pp. 216–34.

———. "Response," *Proceedings of the Rabbinical Assembly of America* 12 (1949), 272–89.

Long, A. A. "Language and Thought in Stoicism," *Problems in Stoicism,* ed. Long. Pp. 75–113.

Mack, Burton L. *"Imitatio Mosis:* Patterns of Cosmology and Soteriology in the Hellenistic Synagogue," *SP* 1 (1972), 27–55.

Marcus, Ralph. "An Outline of Philo's System of Education" (Hebrew), *Sepher Touroff,* eds. I. Silberschlag and J. Twersky. Boston, 1938. Pp. 223–31.

Massebieau, L., and Bréhier, É. "Essai sur la chronologie de la vie et des oeuvres de Philon," *Revue de l'histoire des religions* 53 (1906), 25–64, 164–85, 267–89.

Mayer, G. "Aspekte des Abrahambildes in der hellenistisch-jüdischen Literatur," *Evangelische Theologie* 32 (1972), 118–27.

McKeon, Richard P. "The Liberating and Humanizing Arts in Education," *Humanistic Education and Western Civilization,* ed. A. A. Cohen. New York, 1964. Pp. 159–81.

———. "Rhetoric and Poetic in the Philosophy of Aristotle," *Aristotle's "Poetics" and English Literature,* ed. E. Olson. Chicago, 1965. Pp. 201–36.

Meeks, Wayne A. "The Image of the Androgyne: Some Uses of a Symbol in Earliest Christianity," *History of Religions* 13 (1974), 165–80.

Mendelson, Alan. "A Reappraisal of Wolfson's Method," *SP* 3 (1974–1975), 11–26.

Michel, Alain. "Quelques aspects de la rhétorique chez Philon," *PAL,* 81–101.

Moehring, Horst R. "Arithmology as an Exegetical Tool in the Writings of Philo of Alexandria," Society of Biblical Literature Seminar Papers, I, ed. P. J. Achtemeier. Missoula, 1978. Pp. 191–227.

Montefiore, C. G. "Florilegium Philonis," *JQR* 7 (1895), 481–545.

Mussies, G. "Greek in Palestine and the Diaspora," *The Jewish People in the First Century,* ed. S. Safrai and M. Stern. Vol. 2. Philadelphia, 1976. Pp. 1040–64.

Nock, A. D. "Philo and Hellenistic Philosophy," *Essays on Religion and the Ancient World,* ed. Z. Stewart. 2 vols. Cambridge, 1972. Pp. 559–65.

Pines, S. "The Semantic Distinction between the Terms Astronomy and Astrology according to Al-Bīrūnī," *Isis* 55 (1964), 343–49.

Rijk, L. M. de. *"Enkyklios Paideia:* A Study of Its Original Meaning," *Vivarium* 3 (1965), 24–93.

Robbins, Frank Egleston. "Arithmetic in Philo Judaeus," *CP* 26 (1931), 345–61.

———. "Posidonius and the Sources of Pythagorean Arithmology," *CP* 15 (1920), 309–22.

———. "The Tradition of Greek Arithmology," *CP* 16 (1921), 97–123.

Safrai, S. "Education and the Study of the Torah," *The Jewish People in the First Century,* ed. S. Safrai and M. Stern. Vol. 2. Philadelphia, 1976. Pp. 945–70.

Sandmel, Samuel. "Abraham's Knowledge of the Existence of God," *HTR* 44 (1951), 137–39.

Schwartz, Jacques. "L'Égypte de Philon," *PAL,* 35–44.

Segré, A. "The Status of the Jews in Ptolemaic and Roman Egypt," *Jewish Social Studies* 6 (1944), 375–400.

Shroyer, Montgomery J. "Alexandrian Jewish Literalists," *JBL* 55 (1936), 261–84.

Tcherikover, Victor A. "Jewish Apologetic Literature Reconsidered," *Eos* 48 (1956), 169–93.

Townsend, John T. "Ancient Education in the Time of the Early Roman Empire." *The Catacombs and the Colosseum: The Roman Empire as the Setting of Primitive Christianity,* ed. S. Benko and J. J. O'Rourke. Valley Forge, 1971. Pp. 139–63.

Vermes, G. "The Life of Abraham (1)," *Scripture and Tradition in Judaism.* Leiden, 1961. Ch. 4.

Wacholder, B. Z. "Pseudo-Eupolemos' Two Greek Fragments on the Life of Abraham," *HUCA* 34 (1963), 83–113.

Wagner, W. H. "Philo and *Paideia,*" *Cithara* 10 (1971), 53–64.

Wasserstein, A. "Astronomy and Geometry as Propaedeutic Studies in Rabbinic Literature" (Hebrew), *Tarbiz* 43 (1973–74), 53–57.

Winston, D. "Freedom and Determinism in Greek Philosophy and Jewish Hellenistic Wisdom," *SP* 2 (1973), 23–39.

———. "Freedom and Determinism in Philo of Alexandria," *SP* 3 (1974–75), 47–70.

———. "Was Philo a Mystic?" SBL Seminar Papers (1978). Pp. 161–80.

Index of Passages

184–89	17
194–95	107 n. 12
195	76

De Vita Mosis (Mos.)

i.21–24	4–5
i.23	12, 15, 64, 89 nn. 25, 26, 30
i.25	99 n. 90
i.158–59	63
i.162	53
ii.25–44	83
ii.31–40	xviii
ii.32	82
ii.47–48	63
ii.48	6
ii.124	94 n. 121
ii.126	23, 94 n. 124
ii.211	32, 101 n. 123, 110 n. 7
ii.212	9, 90 n. 57
ii.216	32, 96 n. 44
ii.288	106 n. 85

De Mutatione Nominum (Mut.)

8–10	105 n. 75
10	72
24	102 n. 21
56	38
67	22
76	68
146	37
183	38
211, 218	39
219	103 n. 57
220	109 n. 36
228–29	88 n. 5
229	88 n. 13, 90 n. 36
255ff.	106 n. 96
256	52
256–60	96 n. 45
263	60, 88 n. 13

De Opificio Mundi (Opif.)

passim	xviii, 34, 38
10–11	98 n. 76
23	98 n. 80, 104 n. 64
27	92 n. 96
46	93 n. 104

54–55	35
54–56	107 n. 2
58	94 n. 124, 98 n. 69
58–59	22
69ff.	49, 101 n. 18
69–71	109 n. 30
72	98 n. 68
96	15
103–104	40, 99 n. 86
105	98 n. 85
113	18
128	32
154	89 n. 17
170–72	11

De Plantatione (Plant.).

12	18
14	102 n. 24
26–27	57
80	74
81	38
114	1
127	88 n. 3

De Posteritate Caini (Post.).

52	2
76–78	102 n. 34
97	88 n. 3
101	90 n. 52
118	1
137	88 n. 13, 97 n. 56
138	100 n. 99
140–41	39–40
150	90 n. 57
151–52	38
168–69	105 n. 75
174	64

De Praemiis et Poenis (Praem.)

27	76
29	70
42–44	56–57
43–44	102 n. 28
46	78
62	41
114–15	105 n. 80

Quod Omnis Probus Liber sit (Prob.)

passim	xxv, 6

Classical Authors and Papyri